RECORDING & REPRESENTING KNOWLEDGE

CLASSROOM TECHNIQUES TO HELP STUDENTS ACCURATELY ORGANIZE AND SUMMARIZE CONTENT

D1361725

RECORDING & REPRESENTING KNOWLEDGE

CLASSROOM TECHNIQUES TO HELP STUDENTS ACCURATELY ORGANIZE AND SUMMARIZE CONTENT

Ria A. Schmidt and Robert J. Marzano

With Libby H. Garst and Laurine Halter

Learning Sciences
MARZANO
CENTER

1400 Centrepark Blvd, Suite 1000
West Palm Beach, FL 33401
717-845-6300

email: pub@learningsciences.com
learningsciences.com

Printed in the United States of America

20 19 18 17 16 15   2 3 4

Publisher's Cataloging-in-Publication Data
provided by Five Rainbows Services

Schmidt, Ria A.
  Recording & representing knowledge : classroom techniques to help students accurately organize and summarize content / Ria A. Schmidt [and] Robert J. Marzano.
    pages cm. – (Essentials for achieving rigor series)
  ISBN: 978-1-941112-04-5 (pbk.)
1. Learning strategies. 2. Thought and thinking—Study and teaching. 3. Study skills. 4. Critical thinking—Study and teaching. 5. Learning, Psychology of. I. Marzano, Robert J. II. Title.
  BF441 .S275 2015
  153.4—dc23
                        [2014939202]

MARZANO CENTER

Essentials for Achieving Rigor SERIES

The *Essentials for Achieving Rigor* series of instructional guides helps educators become highly skilled at implementing, monitoring, and adapting instruction. Put it to practical use immediately, adopting day-to-day examples as models for application in your own classroom.

Books in the series:

Identifying Critical Content: Classroom Techniques to Help Students Know What Is Important

Examining Reasoning: Classroom Techniques to Help Students Produce and Defend Claims

Recording & Representing Knowledge: Classroom Techniques to Help Students Accurately Organize and Summarize Content

Examining Similarities & Differences: Classroom Techniques to Help Students Deepen Their Understanding

Processing New Information: Classroom Techniques to Help Students Engage with Content

Revising Knowledge: Classroom Techniques to Help Students Examine Their Deeper Understanding

Practicing Skills, Strategies & Processes: Classroom Techniques to Help Students Develop Proficiency

Engaging in Cognitively Complex Tasks: Classroom Techniques to Help Students Generate & Test Hypotheses across Disciplines

Using Learning Goals & Performance Scales: How Teachers Make Better Instructional Decisions

Organizing for Learning: Classroom Techniques to Help Students Interact within Small Groups

Table of Contents

Acknowledgments..ix

About the Authors.. xi

Introduction 1

Recording and Representing Knowledge........................... 5

PART I
Linguistic Representations..................................... 13

Instructional Technique 1
    Summarizing 15

Instructional Technique 2
    Note Taking 29

PART II
Nonlinguistic Representations.................................. 41

Instructional Technique 3
    Graphic Organizers... 43

Instructional Technique 4
    Pictorial Notes and Pictographs 57

Instructional Technique 5
    Dramatic Enactments....................................... 67

Instructional Technique 6
    Mnemonic Devices 75

Conclusion 85

Resource A Organizer Templates 87

Resource B Helpful Websites 103

References 105

Index 109

Acknowledgments

Learning Sciences International would like to thank the following reviewers:

Kathy Assini
2014 New Jersey Teacher of the Year

Karyn Collie Dickerson
2014 North Carolina Teacher of the Year
Grimsley High School
Greensboro, North Carolina

Michael Lindblad
2015 Oregon Teacher of the Year
Gresham High School/Marylhurst
   University
Gresham, Oregon

Jeri Jo Powers
2008 Kansas Teacher of the Year
Riverview Elementary
Shawnee, Kansas

About the Authors

RIA A. SCHMIDT, PhD, is an educational professional with more than fifteen years of experience as a Teacher, Principal, Central Office Administrator, and Staff Developer. Dr. Schmidt's experience in curriculum and instruction includes creating and presenting professional-development sessions for teachers and administrators on differentiation, rubrics, assessment (formative/summative), proficiency scoring, standards and benchmarks, standards-based education, and standards-based reporting; successfully guiding a school system transition from traditional grading/report cards to a standards-based reporting system; and coordinating standardized assessments and data usage in schools for the purpose of state reporting and informing instruction. In addition, Dr. Schmidt has experience in observing and evaluating both teachers and school administrators.

ROBERT J. MARZANO, PhD, is CEO of Marzano Research Laboratory and Executive Director of the Learning Sciences Marzano Center for Teacher and Leader Evaluation. A leading researcher in education, he is a speaker, trainer, and author of more than 150 articles on topics such as instruction, assessment, writing and implementing standards, cognition, effective leadership, and school intervention. He has authored over 30 books, including *The Art and Science of Teaching* (ASCD, 2007) and *Teacher Evaluation That Makes a Difference* (ASCD, 2013).

LIBBY H. GARST, MSEd, creates professional development for teacher growth as a staff developer and instructional designer for Learning Sciences International and the Marzano Center. She has been a successful teacher and instructional coach. She graduated from Virginia Tech and received her master's degree at the University of Virginia.

LAURINE HALTER, MSEd, has an education career that spans more than 20 years. She has the unique distinction of being awarded the South Dakota Division of Workforce and Career Preparation's Award for Special Educational Programming in Science. She earned her master's degree at South Dakota State University.

Introduction

This guide, *Recording & Representing Knowledge: Classroom Techniques to Help Students Accurately Organize and Summarize Content,* is intended as a resource for improving a specific strategy of instructional practice—recording and representing knowledge.

Your motivation to incorporate this strategy into your instructional toolbox may have come from a personal desire to improve your instructional practice through the implementation of a research-based set of strategies (such as those found in the Marzano instructional framework) or a desire to increase the rigor of the instructional strategies you implement in your classroom so that students meet the expectations of demanding standards such as the Common Core State Standards, Next Generation Science Standards, C3 Framework for Social Studies State Standards, or state standards based on or influenced by College and Career Readiness Anchor Standards.

This guide will help teachers of all grade levels and subjects improve their performance of a specific instructional strategy: recording and representing knowledge. Narrowing your focus on a specific skill, such as recording and representing knowledge, will enable you to more fully understand its complexities to intentionally improve your instruction. Armed with deeper knowledge and practical instructional techniques, you will be able to intentionally plan, implement, monitor, adapt, reflect, and ultimately improve upon the execution of this element of your instructional practice. An individual seeking to become an expert displays distinctive behaviors, as explained by Marzano and Toth (2013):

- breaks down the specific skills required to be an expert

- focuses on improving those particular critical skill chunks (as opposed to easy tasks) during practice or day-to-day activities

- receives immediate, specific, and actionable feedback, particularly from a more experienced coach

- continually practices each critical skill at more challenging levels with the intention of mastering it, giving far less time to skills already mastered

This series of guides will support each of the previously listed behaviors, with a focus on breaking down the specific skills required to be an expert and giving day-to-day practical suggestions to enhance these skills.

Building on the Marzano Instructional Model

This series is based on the Marzano instructional framework, which is grounded in research and provides educators with the tools they need to connect instructional practice to student achievement. The series uses key terms that are specific to the Marzano model of instruction. See Table 1, Glossary of Key Terms.

Table 1: Glossary of Key Terms

Term	Definition
CCSS	Common Core State Standards is the official name of the standards documents developed by the Common Core State Standards Initiative (CCSSI), the goal of which is to prepare students in the United States for college and career.
CCR	College and Career Readiness Anchor Standards are broad statements that incorporate individual standards for various grade levels and specific content areas.
Desired result	The intended result for the student(s) due to the implementation of a specific strategy.
Monitoring	The act of checking for evidence of the desired result of a specific strategy while the strategy is being implemented.
Instructional strategy	A category of techniques used for classroom instruction that has been proven to have a high probability of enhancing student achievement.
Instructional technique	The method used to teach and deepen understanding of knowledge and skills.
Content	The knowledge and skills necessary for students to demonstrate standards.
Scaffolding	A purposeful progression of support that targets cognitive complexity and student autonomy to reach rigor.
Extending	Activities that move students who have already demonstrated the desired result to a higher level of understanding.

The educational pendulum swings widely from decade to decade. Educators move back and forth between prescriptive checklists and step-by-step lesson plans to approaches that encourage instructional autonomy with minimal regard for the science of teaching and need for accountability. Two practices are often missing in both of these approaches to defining effective instruction: 1) specific statements of desired results, and 2) solid research-based connections. The Marzano instructional framework provides a comprehensive system that details what is required from teachers to develop their craft using research-based instructional strategies. Launching from this solid instructional foundation, teachers will then be prepared to merge that science with their own unique, yet effective, instructional style, which is the art of teaching.

Recording & Representing Knowledge: Classroom Techniques to Help Students Accurately Organize and Summarize Content will help you grow into an innovative and highly skilled teacher who is able to implement, scaffold, and extend instruction to meet a range of student needs.

Essentials for Achieving Rigor

This series of guides details essential classroom strategies to support the complex shifts in teaching that are necessary for an environment where academic rigor is a requirement for all students. The instructional strategies presented in this series are essential to effectively teach the CCSS, the Next Generation Science Standards, or standards designated by your school district or state. They require a deeper understanding, more effective use of strategies, and greater frequency of implementation for your students to demonstrate the knowledge and skills required by rigorous standards. This series includes instructional techniques appropriate for all grade levels and content areas. The examples contained within are grade-level specific and should serve as models and launching points for application in your own classroom.

Your skillful implementation of these strategies is essential to your students' mastery of CCSS or other rigorous standards, no matter the grade level or subject matter you are teaching. Other instructional strategies covered in the Essentials for Achieving Rigor series, such as examining reasoning and engaging students in cognitively complex tasks, exemplify the cognitive complexity needed to meet rigorous standards. Taken as a package, these strategies may at first glance seem quite daunting. For this reason, the series focuses on just one strategy in each guide.

Recording and Representing Knowledge

Recording and representing knowledge is a powerful instructional strategy that is essential for your students' acquisition, organization, and retention of content knowledge. This strategy offers multiple ways for students to record and represent new knowledge in either linguistic or nonlinguistic forms. Whenever you present new critical content, take time to identify the most efficient way to show your students how to record and represent that knowledge and intentionally make it part of your lesson plan.

Recording knowledge is the first aspect of this instructional strategy. When students record knowledge, they write down words or phrases about the central ideas and important details of content in their own words. These summaries are called linguistic representations. The second aspect of the strategy, representing knowledge, occurs when students translate new information into nonlinguistic representations such as graphic organizers, pictorial notes and pictographs, dramatic enactments, or mnemonics.

The Effective Implementation of Recording and Representing Knowledge

To effectively implement recording and representing knowledge, students must be able to summarize what they have learned. This entails being able to put information they have heard or read into their own words or into the form of a nonlinguistic representation such as a graphic organizer, dramatic enactment, or picture. Summarization, whether for recording or representing knowledge, requires that students process what they have heard or read, analyze that information, identify the critical content, and assimilate this critical content in a meaningful way. Only at that point will they be ready to record or represent their new learning.

Irrespective of your students' grade levels or the difficulty of the content they are expected to master, many of them are no doubt stuck at a very basic level of summarizing. They need some techniques for summarizing. You will find them in this guide. The following teacher behaviors are associated with the effective implementation of recording and representing knowledge:

- teaching and showing students how to summarize new critical content

- teaching and showing students how to generate notes that identify critical information in the content

- teaching and showing students how to use graphic organizers to demonstrate relationships or patterns in their knowledge

- teaching and showing students how to use dramatic enactments, such as role plays, scenes, processes, events, or alternative methods, to symbolize the content in some manner

- teaching and showing students how to use mnemonic devices, such as rhymes, acronyms, and songs, to aid them in the retention and recall of important information

As you prepare to effectively implement this strategy, think first about how to avoid the following common mistakes. These roadblocks can take your teaching, and ultimately your students' learning, off course:

- The teacher fails to give students the time to frequently record and represent.

- The teacher fails to let students think for themselves.

- The teacher fails to use an appropriate method for recording or representing.

Failing to Give Students Frequent Opportunities to Record and Represent Knowledge

With the pressure you feel to cover content standards, you can easily become caught up in the frantic presentation of new information and fail to give students the time they need to process and elaborate content in advance of recording or representing their understanding of their new knowledge. The desired result of recording and representing knowledge is that students will be able to understand and retain content knowledge in accurate ways. If your students have shallow or no background knowledge about a subject or if the content is particularly difficult, give students frequent opportunities to process, elaborate, record, or represent. You might implement this cycle after every chunk of new material is presented. A rule of thumb for the frequency of recording and representing is this: The more familiar students are with the content and the easier the content is, the less often they will need to record or represent.

Failing to Let Students Think for Themselves

In the past, the common practice was to provide the notes (summaries, concepts, interpreted information) for students, and they would then memorize what they recorded in order to answer questions on a unit test. However, gone are the days of asking students to "copy the notes from the board." Recording and representing knowledge requires students to do both thinking and recording and representing. It is during this process that they gain a deeper understanding and retain the critical information.

Failing to Use an Appropriate Method for Recording and Representing

As you will discover while reading this guide, there are many ways students can record and represent knowledge, but some are more appropriate for recording certain types of information. For example, one of the best ways to aid retention of a list of information is through using mnemonic devices. Using a graphic organizer may not be as effective in helping students retain a set of discrete facts that need to be recalled instantly. Consider the type of information being taught, evaluate the best uses of each technique for recording and representing that information, and then pair your content with the appropriate technique.

Monitoring for the Desired Result

The effective implementation of recording and representing knowledge involves more than just giving students opportunities for summarizing, note taking, and creating graphic organizers. It requires monitoring for the desired result of that strategy in real time. Presenting a lively lesson with multiple "bells and whistles" is not enough. The essential question is, did your students learn or master the information taught? A more specific question is, was the desired result of the strategy achieved? The most elaborately planned lessons can be exercises in futility unless they begin with instructional strategies in mind, focus on standards, and are monitored by the teacher for the desired results.

There are several ways teachers can monitor whether students are effectively recording and representing knowledge. Following are the main pieces of evidence that can tell you if your students are able to derive meaning from the content in a specific lesson:

- When prompted, students can identify and explain the main points of a lesson.

- Organization and summarization of important content is evident in student work.

- Organization and summarization of important content is evident in student discussions.

- Student linguistic representations—such as notes and academic notebooks—include critical content.

- Student nonlinguistic representations—such as graphic organizers, pictorial notes, pictographs, dramatic enactments, and mnemonic devices—accurately represent critical content.

- Students record and represent knowledge without prompting from the teacher and seek adaptations when necessary.

Each technique discussed in this guide contains examples of monitoring specific to that technique.

Scaffolding and Extending Instruction to Meet Students' Needs

As you monitor for the desired result of each technique, you will no doubt realize that some students are unable to identify the critical content, while others are easily able to demonstrate the desired result. With this knowledge, it becomes necessary to adapt for the needs of your students. There are four different categories of support you can provide for students who need scaffolding: 1) support that teachers (including instructional aides or other paraprofessionals) or peers provide; 2) support that teachers provide by manipulating the difficulty level of content that is being taught (e.g., providing an easier reading level that contains the same content); 3) breaking down the content into smaller chunks to make it more manageable; and 4) giving students organizers or think sheets to clarify and guide their thinking through a task one step at a time (Dickson, Collins, Simmons & Kame'enui, 1998).

Within each technique that is described in this guide, you will find examples of ways to scaffold and extend instruction to meet the needs of your students. Scaffolding provides support that targets cognitive complexity and student autonomy and rigor. Extending moves students who have already demonstrated the desired result to a higher level of understanding. These examples are provided as suggestions and you should adapt them to target the specific needs of your students. Use the scaffolding examples to spark ideas as you plan to meet the needs of your English-language learners, students who receive special education or lack support, or simply the student who was absent the day before. The extension activities can help you plan for students in your gifted and talented program or those with a keen interest in the subject matter you are teaching who have already learned the fundamentals.

Teacher Self-Reflection

As you develop expertise in teaching students to record and represent knowledge, reflecting on your skill level and effectiveness can help you become more successful in implementing this strategy. Use the following set of reflection questions to guide you. The questions begin simply, with reflecting on how to start the implementation process, and move to progressively more complex ways of helping students record and represent knowledge.

1. How can you incorporate some aspect of this strategy in your instruction?

2. How can you engage students in activities that help them record and represent their knowledge and understanding of important content using a variety of models?

3. How can you monitor the extent to which recording and representing knowledge enhances student understanding?

4. How might you adapt and create new strategies for recording and representing knowledge that address unique student needs and situations?

5. What are you learning about your students as you adapt and create new strategies?

Instructional Techniques to Help Students Record and Represent Knowledge

There are many ways to help your students effectively record and represent knowledge with the ultimate goal being their mastery of the learning targets of your grade level or content. The approaches you choose to use during a specific lesson or unit will depend on the grade you teach, content involved, and makeup of your class. These various approaches are called instructional techniques. In this guide, they are divided into two categories—linguistic and nonlinguistic representations. The following pages provide descriptions of how to implement the techniques in each category:

Part I: Linguistic Representations

Instructional Technique 1: Summarizing

Instructional Technique 2: Note Taking

Part II: Nonlinguistic Representations

Instructional Technique 3: Graphic Organizers

Instructional Technique 4: Pictorial Notes and Pictographs

Instructional Technique 5: Dramatic Enactments

Instructional Technique 6: Mnemonic Devices

All of the techniques are similarly organized and include the following components:

- a brief introduction to the technique

- ways to effectively implement the technique

- common mistakes to avoid as you implement the technique

- examples and nonexamples from elementary and secondary class-rooms using selected learning targets or standards from various documents

- ways to monitor for the desired result

- a scale for monitoring students

- ways to scaffold and extend instruction to meet the needs of students

PART I

LINGUISTIC REPRESENTATIONS

Linguistic, or semantic, representations are the most well-known and commonly used methods for students to .record what they have learned, either from lesson presentations or independent reading. Just ahead in Part I, you will find two linguistic techniques to help you teach your students how to first summarize critical content from classroom presentations or the reading of text (Instructional Technique 1) and then take meaningful notes to further their understanding and retention of content (Instructional Technique 2).

Instructional Technique 1

SUMMARIZING

Summarizing is an essential skill for students if they are to write down the essence of what they have learned. Before students can take accurate and useful notes, they must be able to summarize. However, simply telling students to write a summary without directly instructing them how to do it, as well as modeling the process for them, is like telling someone who does not know how to ride a two-wheeled bicycle to jump on the newest model and ride to the park.

There are three levels of cognitive complexity in summarization: 1) *retrieval*, in which students write about critical content using written clues and prompts provided by the teacher; 2) *comprehension*, in which students write about critical content in their own words demonstrating a deeper understanding; and 3) *analysis*, in which students restate, in their own words, the main message of critical content in a succinct sentence and relate supporting details from a classroom lesson or text.

How to Effectively Implement Summarizing

The effective implementation of summarizing depends on your ability to teach directly what summarizing is and then model the process for your students as appropriate to your content and grade level. Following are several approaches to teaching summarizing.

Teach the Action Verbs of Summarizing

As noted, summarizing is a complex process involving multiple cognitive actions. Once you understand the actions that comprise summarizing, you can more readily teach and model them for your students. Here are the action verbs: 1) *comprehend*, 2) *chunk*, 3) *compact*, 4) *conceptualize*, and 5) *connect*. Each of these requires the learner to assume a different perspective on the text or a teacher presentation. The actions are described just ahead. As you read through the descriptions, assess how well your students might be able to implement any of the actions. For a student to implement the whole summarizing package below, he must be a highly skilled reader who has a great deal of background knowledge. Though these are in step-by-step order, choose a single aspect of this package that might be a starting point for helping your students improve their summarizing expertise.

1. *Comprehension:* This creates the biggest stumbling block for learners at any level whether they are elementary students or graduate school PhD candidates. Learners cannot create summaries before they actually understand what they have heard or read. A good test for whether your students truly comprehend is to ask them to explain the critical content in a sentence or two to you or classmates. If students can't explain it, they need to go back and reread the text, ask questions about what they don't understand, figure out the meaning of new vocabulary, talk about the information with a partner, or find some other sources of information to help them make sense of it. Students must process the new content in some way for them to understand it. This important step of comprehension is laid out in the learning target: *Read closely to determine what the text says explicitly* (CCSS ELA & Literacy, CCR Anchor Standard 1 for Reading). This expectation may require multiple readings of critical content to reach the level of comprehension required for summarization.

2. *Chunking:* When you are presenting new content to students, you will likely make the decisions about how to chunk content. After presenting one chunk of important information, resist the temptation to press on, and stop talking. Give students an opportunity to think, pair, and share about what you have said and then jot down some notes about what is most important. When students are reading text with summarization as a goal, chunking that text into logical parts can reduce the frustration of trying to remember everything at once.

3. *Compacting:* This process takes text or a teacher's lecture with hundreds of words and multiple concepts and details and shrinks it down, or compacts it, into a neat and tidy package. Skilled readers and listeners learn to recognize the central idea and important details. They are also able to ignore trivial and unimportant information (this is not to say that the trivial and unimportant information might not be

interesting to read). But, students can't remember everything. Model for your students how a skilled reader actually determines when information is worthy of being included in a summary. However, skilled readers learn that when they are taking notes and creating a summary, it must also contain a simple statement in their own words.

4. *Conceptualizing:* This takes some practice, but once students have seen you model it several times, they will begin to come up with key words and ideas from a chunk of text or lesson presentation.

5. *Connecting:* If your complete presentation or total text is composed of—for example—three chunks, students will have recorded three sets of words or phrases all related to the overall topic of the presentation or the text. The challenge now is for the students to play with these three phrases or words to produce a summary sentence.

Table 1.1 presents the five steps and their student-friendly definitions. If you feel confident about your students' abilities to swallow and digest these steps all at once, take the plunge. However, keep in mind that you will have to polish up your own summarizing skills to model for students the steps one at a time in relatively student-friendly text. If you can't do it, don't expect your students to do it.

Table 1.1: Five Action Verbs for Summarizing

Step	Action to Be Taken
Comprehend	Read and understand the text.
Chunk	Divide it into parts. If you are reading a long text, try to divide it into more manageable chunks.
Compact	Make the text shorter by collapsing lists and deleting unimportant information.
Conceptualize	Think of a key word or phrase that sums up each chunk.
Connect	Combine the key words and phrases from each chunk into a summary sentence.

Teach Critical Content While Facilitating Summarizing

The lesson plan for presenting content while facilitating summarizing, presented in Table 1.2, assumes that you have directly taught and modeled summarizing using small chunks of text, particularly the action of conceptualizing (i.e., choosing key words and phrases from the presentation or text). Students are beginning to assume more responsibility for doing their own thinking, but they may still need facilitation. Facilitation is the process of thinking along with students and helping them develop their own ideas. Rather than managing students' thinking and overexplaining ideas, or telling students what to do and how to do it, encourage and question. Using this lesson, expect students to assume more responsibility for summarizing as you prompt them to listen for key words and phrases rather than identify them during the reading of text.

Table 1.2: A Lesson Plan for Presenting Critical Content While Facilitating Summarization

Step	Process
Identify the critical content you plan to teach. Chunk the critical content into three equal parts. Divide your presentation into three ten-minute segments. Either prepare a template on which students can record their key words and phrases or direct them to divide a sheet of notebook paper into three sections.	Resist the temptation to continue talking longer than ten minutes. Plan this lesson so that each ten-minute segment is packed with critical content. There will be no room for tangents or distractions in your presentation.
Present the first chunk of the lesson to students.	Students should be in the listening mode with their pencils down, leaving their minds free to engage with what you are saying. Encourage them to listen for key words or phrases. If they think of something to write down, encourage them to be disciplined enough to wait a few minutes. If they start writing while you are still talking, they may miss a very important idea or detail.
At the end of the first chunk, ask students to quickly write down the key words or phrases that seemed to summarize the critical content you presented. Once they have written their phrases, direct them to talk with their partners about what they thought and why.	Encourage the partners to talk about why they chose the key words or phrases they did. Walk around the room to listen in on what students are saying or check for what they have written. Another way to check for understanding is to ask students to write their key words or phrases on their whiteboards and hold them up.
Present the second chunk of the lesson to students.	Again, resist the temptation to talk for more than ten minutes.

Step	Process
At the end of this chunk, direct students to work with their assigned partner to make a list of any key words or phrases they heard that contained important information.	Keep a close eye on partners who are having difficulty, and provide some prompts or questions to get them moving. In this part of the lesson, resist the temptation to give students answers in order to fill in the blanks. Hold students accountable for thinking.
Go through the process of presenting and stopping to process one last time.	Now is the time for students to assemble their final set of key words and phrases. Encourage the partners to talk about the choices they have made. Students can certainly modify their word or phrase choices during this discussion.
Make certain that you have provided adequate modeling of this step. The final connecting/combining of the key words and phrases into a summary sentence is the most challenging for students.	If you have not adequately modeled this final connecting step, choose one set of partners to write their key words and phrases on the board. Then model for them several different ways their key ideas and details might combine to make a good sentence. This is an experimental process where you combine some key words and read them aloud to see how they sound. If the partner pair that you chose did not do an adequate job of selecting key ideas and details, take this opportunity to discuss with students how important their listening and thinking skills are to writing a good summary. If they do not select the central ideas and key details, they will not be able to write a good summary. Elicit some more appropriate key words and phrases, and show students how much easier it is to write a summary if they have actually listened and made good word choices.

Teach the Independent Reading of Content Text While Facilitating Summarization

You can adapt the previous process for facilitating summarizing in the presentation of a content lesson to facilitating summarizing during the reading of text. There are several ways to structure the reading, but the first time you use this approach, implement partner choral reading. Using this method ensures that all students are processing the text, and when they finish their reading of the first chunk of text, they can immediately begin discussing the central ideas and important details. Table 1.3 provides a brief lesson plan for teaching independent reading of content text by facilitating summarizing.

Table 1.3: A Lesson Plan for Teaching the Reading of Content Text While Facilitating Summarization

Step	Description
Choose the content text you want students to read. Chunk it into three manageable sections.	If you are going to use this lesson plan on future occasions, prepare a template on which students can write their names, the names of their partners, and the key words and phrases they identify for each of the chunks they read. Give each set of partners one of the organizers.
Instruct students on how to engage in partner choral reading. Give each set of partners a reasonable amount of time to finish the reading. Because it is oral reading, most pairs should be finished at about the same time.	In partner choral reading, students read aloud with a partner. They set the speed and work together to make it sound as one voice. Each set of partners will be reading the same text.
Direct students to talk with their partners about which ideas, details, key words, and phrases come to their minds after their reading. Remind them that they will be asked to write a summary of the entire text after they read two more chunks.	Give students an adequate amount of time to process and discuss the text with partners. Direct students to write the key words and phrases they identified from the first chunk of text on their organizer.
Give students another reasonable period of time to read and adequately process the second chunk of text.	Direct students to write their key words and phrases they identified from their second chunk of text on their organizer.
Direct students to talk with their partners as before. Remind them to be thinking about whether this second chunk gave them any additional information. Remind them to ignore any unimportant information.	Continually monitor students' processing and recording.
Using the same steps as earlier, complete the reading of the third chunk.	Continually walk around and monitor while students are chorally reading to ensure that all students are fully invested in processing the text.
If you have modeled the process of combining key words and phrases from several chunks of text in a summary statement, direct your students to use that process to produce a summary statement.	If students are not ready to write their own summary at this point, model the process for them using the key words and phrases generated by the students.

Teach Various Prompts and Processes for Summarizing

Teaching students how to summarize begins in preschool and kindergarten. At those levels students do less recording and more representing. However, by the time students are in first grade or even earlier, they can already record knowledge. It's up to you to teach them how to summarize during the recording process. The earlier they begin to think in terms of summarizing whenever they hear a story read aloud or whenever the teacher explains something important, the more readily it will become a habit of the mind that follows them throughout middle and high school as well as college and career. Following are some examples of prompts and processes you can use to scaffold summarizing for younger or struggling students.

Somebody-Wanted-But-So-Then (SWBST)

This set of prompts helps students write a simple summary sentence about a story they have read or a section of a textbook that features a historical figure. To create a SWBST organizer, use the landscape view of a sheet of blank paper and divide it into four columns. Write the words *somebody, wanted,* and *but* at the top of the first three columns. Write the phrase *so then* at the top of the fourth column. After students hear a story read aloud or read the story independently, have them fill in the information from the story or content. The final step involves combining the key words and phrases to form a summary sentence. For example, students read the fairy tale *The Emperor's New Clothes.* The teacher works with them to fill in each column with the appropriate information. Here's what the teacher and class came up with for their final summary statement: *The Emperor wanted outfits that would be invisible to people who weren't fit for their jobs, but he didn't realize that the weavers were only pretending to weave cloth, so (then) he was humiliated by appearing in public without any clothes on.* The SWBST sentences can get a little cumbersome, but this organizer is a good first step to understanding what a summary is all about.

Get the Gist

Getting the gist of something is a quick way of describing that an individual has figured out the big idea of a story, presentation, TV show, or movie. The term *gist* is the point or central idea. Using this approach, students determine the who, what, when, where, why, and how of a concept or chunk of text. They then use those notes to write a twenty-word summary called a gist.

Students can use this strategy for content-area texts to aid in their comprehension and summarizing skills. (See a template for the Get the Gist organizer in Resource A.1.)

Summary Frames

Summary frames are a series of prompts that the teacher can provide orally but are most commonly listed in a worksheet format. The questions can help students retrieve the critical content from a chunk of information the teacher presents or a text that the student is independently reading. Students write short answers to the questions and then a summary based on their responses. There are many types of summary frames, such as argumentation frame, definition frame, problem/solution frame, topic-restriction-illustration frame, conversation frame, and narrative frame. (See Resource A.2 for a narrative frame template.)

Common Mistakes

Following are a few of the common mistakes teachers can make as they teach and model summarizing for their students:

- The teacher does not directly teach and model the process of summarizing for students before expecting them to write summaries independently.

- The teacher does not allocate appropriate amounts of instructional time to teach and model summarizing.

- The teacher does not break down the various aspects of summarizing into manageable chunks of instruction.

- The teacher chooses text that is too difficult for students to read and comprehend.

- The teacher develops the summary and dictates it to students.

- The teacher fails to gradually release the responsibility of summarizing to students.

Examples and Nonexamples of Summarizing

These examples and nonexamples may be from a different grade level or subject than you teach. View them as a fresh perspective from a colleague, and use them to develop a new approach or alternative way of thinking about how you will directly teach and show your students how to summarize.

Elementary Example of Summarizing

The first example illustrates how and how not to teach and model summarizing in a second-grade class. The learning target being addressed is this: *Identify the main topic of a multiparagraph text as well as the focus of specific paragraphs within the text* (see also CCSS ELA & Literacy, Reading–Informational Text Grades K–5). Students are reading from their social studies textbook. The teacher has previously taught students the term *main topic* using the definition "what a whole article or story is mainly about." She has also introduced students to the term focus, defining *focus* as "what a paragraph in a whole article is specifically about."

To accomplish the goal set forth in the learning target, the teacher decides to use a modified version of the lesson plan found in Table 1.3. Her students are accustomed to working with their partners to discuss passages they have chorally read together. This methodology ensures that all students are personally processing the text.

> Boys and girls, today we are going to continue practicing an important reading skill: looking for main topics while we read. Who can tell me what a main topic is? Jeremy, I saw you look over at the Definition Chart. Read it for us, please. *Jeremy reads, "The main topic is what a short story or article is mainly about."* Let me give you an example of how this works. Suppose we're reading an article about desert animals. The first paragraph describes some of the animals that live in the desert. The second paragraph describes some of the special ways those animals survive the heat and drought in the desert. The last paragraph tells us what we can learn from desert animals about surviving in the desert. *The teacher creates a numbered list and then queries the students for the*

focus of each paragraph. What was the first paragraph about? Write the correct answer on your whiteboards. Desert animals. How about the second paragraph? How the animals adapt to the desert. How about the third paragraph? How we can adapt to the desert using what we learn from animals. There are two important questions I want you to answer for me now. First, what was the main topic of that three-paragraph article? Explain to your partner how you know that you have identified the main topic. *The teacher walks around and listens for students to articulate the idea that each paragraph was focused on or described some details about the main topic.* What was the focus of the first paragraph? Right, descriptions of some of the animals that live there. That was the focus of the first paragraph. Now, tell me the focus of the second paragraph. And the third.

Satisfied that her students have fully understood the process, the teacher asks them to turn to a three-paragraph section in their social studies book that she has selected for them to read. She provides a brief organizer for students to complete during their reading: main topic of the section, focus of the first paragraph, focus of the second paragraph, and focus of the third paragraph. Partners read the first paragraph chorally and agree on the focus. Partners repeat this process until they have read all three paragraphs and identified a focus for each one. Then, they identify the main topic of all three paragraphs.

Elementary Nonexample of Summarizing

The nonexample teacher has the same general plan as the example teacher. However, the nonexample teacher is anxious to have her students read their social studies book. She doesn't give them a brief explanation with examples of how one makes a decision about the main topic of a three-paragraph story and the focus on each paragraph. The teacher has neither taught nor modeled for her students how to summarize, one of the most common mistakes you can make when expecting students to do so.

Secondary Example of Summarizing

The secondary example takes place in a high school English class. The learning target is: *Determine the central ideas or themes of a text and analyze their development; summarize the key supporting details and ideas* (CCSS ELA & Literacy, CCR Anchor Standard 2 for Reading). The teacher selects an approach called a snapshot summary (McEwan-Adkins & Burnett, 2013) that uses picture taking as a metaphor. The metaphor is an apt one since almost all of her students are constantly snapping pictures of their friends and family.

The term *snapshot summary* captures the essence of what she is asking them to do as they read text in her classroom. She has carefully chosen the text she asks her students to read and divides it into three chunks. She first defines for her students what a snapshot summary is: a sentence or phrase you write that states the central idea of one chunk of text. Here's how she introduces her lesson.

> Good morning, class. Today, we're going to be creating snapshot summaries. Tell me what comes to your mind when you hear that phrase. *A student says he's keeping a snapshot summary of his day and invites the teacher to pose for a picture as he takes out his cell phone.* Well, a snapshot summary isn't a photo. It's a summary that captures in words the essence of something you've read, just like your photo captures the moment you're having with friends or family. Let me give you my definition of a snapshot summary: a sentence or phrase you write that states the central idea of one chunk of text.

The teacher hands out copies of the three-paragraph text the students will be reading and also an organizer on which to record their snapshot summaries. After students have chorally read the first chunk of text with their partners, the teacher models for them how she would choose the key words or phrases for her snapshot summary of that chunk. She writes her chosen key words and phrases on the SMART Board in the appropriate spot on the organizer. After students chorally read the second chunk of text, the teacher asks for volunteers to work with her to describe how they would create a snapshot summary statement for the second chunk of text. Then she directs them to chorally read the third chunk of text, process it with their partners, and write a snapshot summary for it. At that point in the lesson, the teacher decides to wait until the next day to model for students how to combine their snapshot summaries into a one-sentence summary that states the central idea of the text.

Secondary Nonexample of Summarizing

The nonexample teacher tells her students to read the three-paragraph article and write some short key words and phrases to describe each paragraph. Then she instructs them to combine these key words and phrases to write a one-sentence summary of the full text. She doesn't model the process for her students, nor does she give them a chance to work collaboratively in either a whole group discussion or with partners. They are expected to complete the work with very little direction and support from either their classmates or teacher. Many students are frustrated and unable to finish the assignment.

Determining If Students Can Summarize Critical Content

Monitoring your students' mastery of summarizing is an ongoing and sometimes frustrating experience. The degree of success students have when they summarize is heavily dependent on the difficulty level of the text they are reading and the amount of prior knowledge students have about a given topic or process. Here are some examples of monitoring that will allow you to assess whether students are achieving the desired result of your instruction and serve as cues that you may need to step back and provide more scaffolding for some students:

- Students discuss with partners the steps in the process of summarizing as the teacher moves quickly about the room and listens for their understanding of the process.

- Students write summaries of a classroom discussion of text and give them to the teacher as their exit ticket. The teacher reads the summaries later and makes notes about students' progress and where reteaching or additional modeling may be required.

The student proficiency scale for summarizing in Table 1.4 shows the range of student proficiencies for how successfully students are able to summarize the critical content of a specific lesson or text.

Table 1.4: Student Proficiency Scale for Summarizing

Emerging	Fundamental	Desired Result
Students are able to summarize critical content using written cues and prompts provided by the teacher. Students are unable to generate notes that summarize the critical information in the lesson without help from a peer partner or the teacher.	Students can write a summary of critical content in their own words that restates the central idea. Students can write a summary that includes some but not all of the supporting details. Students are unable to create a succinct summary.	Students can write a succinct summary sentence of critical content in their own words that restates the central idea and supporting details from a classroom lesson or independent reading. Students are able to explain their summarization of critical information to peers or the teacher.

Scaffold and Extend Instruction to Meet Students' Needs

There will be many students who are not able to readily summarize. Their difficulties lie, for the most part, in the area of comprehension. As stated earlier in this section, if students cannot understand what they have read, they will be unable to summarize it. There are other students who may readily comprehend but be unable to expertly use the cognitive process of summarizing. There are fewer students than you might think who need extended instruction, but you should anticipate their needs as you plan.

Scaffolding

Here are some ways to scaffold summarization instruction:

- Use text that is at the students' reading level.

- Use a variety of prompts to scaffold the summarizing process.

- Ask students probing questions to help them articulate their own learning.

- Prepare a chart to help students evaluate their summaries. This chart would contain the following statements: *A summary is short. A summary leaves out unimportant details. A summary doesn't copy or retell the story. A summary tells what is most important.* Post the chart where students can refer to it as necessary, and use it to teach a mini-lesson to struggling students. Encourage them to use the statements to evaluate their own summaries.

- Summarize events, classroom happenings, and day-to-day routines so that students have constant opportunities to summarize "easy information."

- Provide peer support for reading more challenging classroom text in the form of choral reading or audiobooks.

- Give students extra time to both think and work.

Extending

Here are some ways to extend summarizing for students who have achieved the desired result:

- Notch up the difficulty of the content text or provide primary and secondary sources for students to summarize for classmates who are unable to read them independently.

- Assign students to provide one-sentence model summaries such as those that appear in *The New York Times* Sunday Book Review or Best Sellers report. The summaries students prepare could help other students in the class choose books for recreational reading.

Instructional Technique 2

NOTE TAKING

Note taking is a powerful learning tool that students can use to record information a teacher presents orally or visually (PowerPoint slides, videos, films, demonstrations, experiments, or artifacts) to record central ideas and key details from text that they are reading. The "when" and "how" of the note taking will dictate the degree of benefit that your students receive from the activity. There is nothing magical in note taking that transforms the words on the page to ideas, concepts, and summaries. For example, if students merely copy words by rote from either the board or text, they can copy several paragraphs without understanding a word they have written. This principle also applies when students are attempting to write down every word the teacher utters while the teacher is talking. This classroom version of court reporting may look impressive since students seem highly engaged and have the written work to prove it. However, their experience is akin to shooting a video of a parade or a family gathering and not being able to remember anything that happened at the event. In the act of recording something at the same time it is happening, one can easily miss the opportunity to emotionally and intellectually engage with what is taking place, or in the case of note taking, to pick up key ideas and details. The benefits of note taking can be realized only when learners understand the concept of summarizing as described in the first technique, understand precisely when and why they are to take notes, and are able to independently generate a simple summary of a central idea supported by key details.

How to Effectively Implement Note Taking

Students can take notes in a variety of formats to be discussed just ahead. You may already have a preferred note-taking method that you use in your classroom. The methodology you use is not as critical as how you choose to directly instruct and show your students how the note-taking method works. Here are some guidelines to follow:

1. Teach the method to students at the beginning of the school year with many examples and daily practice exercises in the case of more complex methods until they understand the method and are able to make it a routine.

2. Consistently use the method on a daily basis.

3. Collect, read, and comment on notes to keep students accountable.

4. Use the notes to inform your lesson planning and also to dictate the need for scaffolding and extending for specific students.

To summarize, the effective implementation of note taking is dependent on your commitment to teaching and modeling your preferred method for students at the beginning of the school year and consistently monitoring the implementation to make sure that everyone is on board. Following are several note-taking approaches to consider if you have never implemented a standard note-taking procedure for your students: 1) informal outlines, 2) teacher-designed templates, and 3) dual formats such as free-flowing webs, combination notes, and academic notebooks.

Informal Outlines

One of the most common note-taking techniques is the informal outline. Students determine the most critical pieces of information they should include, and those become the left-most headings in the outline. If needed, these points can be broken down into more detailed sections that support the bigger ideas. Indentation is used to indicate the relative importance of the information. See Table 1.5 in the secondary classroom example of note taking.

Teacher-Designed Templates

You may have experimented with and ultimately discarded expert-recommended formats, but you chose to design your own note-taking format. If it works for you and enables your students to record and represent their knowledge in a systematic way that achieves the desired result, you are to be commended.

Dual-Format Note-Taking Methods

Dual-format note-taking methods give students an opportunity to process content from lesson presentations or text in both linguistic and nonlinguistic formats. The following methods range from a simple and very easy-to-use free-flowing web appropriate even for preschool and kindergarten students, to the complex and multidimensional academic notebook that is most suited for secondary students. Between these two approaches is the combination-notes approach, a simple one-page format that provides spaces for students to summarize their learning after writing down notes and drawing pictorial representations.

Free-Flowing Web

Later, in one of the classroom examples, you will find a sample free-flowing web students created. At first glance, it may appear to be nothing more than a simple graphic organizer. However, what distinguishes this web from traditional graphic organizers discussed later in this guide is its "free-flowing" character. It can be anything and go anywhere. No specific number of circles is required, and the information recorded is what students have gleaned from their processing and elaborating. There are no frames (labels) dictating what kind of information must be placed in the circle.

To create free-flowing webs, students draw circles and straight lines to form a web that represents critical information from text or a lesson presentation. For example, students might begin their free-flowing web with a large circle and write the most important concept or idea in that circle. The disadvantage of this technique is that students are somewhat limited in the amount of information they can record. This type of note taking is ideal for younger students. At the outset, the teacher can identify the big idea, and students can add details or pictorial notes in smaller circles. See Figure 2.1 in the elementary classroom example just ahead in this section.

Combination Notes

Combination notes actually fit in both the linguistic- and nonlinguistic-representation categories because they combine both types of methods. In this approach to note taking, students use a two-column format to record written notes about both the content and the nonlinguistic representations, such as pictographs or diagrams, to demonstrate their learning. (See Resource A.3 for a combination-notes template.)

Academic Notebooks

Academic notebooks are designed to contain a permanent record of students' analyses and syntheses of the content they have learned. Students date their entries in the notebook, which include generated notes, reactions to content, questions and answers, and reflections on their progress. They might also include things they want to know or questions from that day's experience. In their academic notebooks, students can include most of the methods of linguistic or nonlinguistic representation that are covered in this guide. That is why they are designated as a dual-format approach to taking notes. However, academic notebooks go far beyond the other approaches to note taking. The benefits of teaching students how to construct an academic notebook include the following:

- Students have a permanent record of their initial thinking.

- Students have a sequential record of their understanding.

- Students can refine and advance their thinking as you implement other instructional strategies covered in the Essentials for Achieving Rigor series such as examining reasoning and revising knowledge.

- Instruct and model for students how to use and organize their academic notebooks. You cannot expect most students to be organized if you do not provide several accurate models for them: 1) an example of what the academic notebook should look like right down to the color-coded folders and color-coding labeling system; 2) a demonstration of how to put the notebook together in which students have all of the pieces, and you walk them through the process of constructing the notebook; and 3) a notebook that students developed during a previous school year.

- If you have never used academic notebooks, you may need to construct a sample day of notebook notes out of thin air, hoping that you accurately represent something you have never fully experienced from the students' perspective. If you are an experienced teacher and have used academic notebooks for many years, you can no doubt borrow an outstanding example from a former student to show your current students. Here are some common aspects of an academic notebook: 1) blank or preformatted pages for taking notes, writing reflections in a journal, drawings, and graphic organizers; and 2) a color-coding and labeling system (revise content in blue ink, highlight questions in yellow, underline critical content in red ink, etc.) that the teacher predetermines. Students date their entries to serve as a timeline of learning. In addition to notes, students can add reflection entries in the notebook to help them understand their thinking at the time.

- One important advantage of implementing academic notebooks is the opportunity they provide for students to examine their reasoning and revise knowledge. Students need to be given time to go back to their academic notebooks to revise and update the notes they took after the initial critical-input experience. Remember that during the note-taking experience, students do not need to be completely accurate in their understanding of the critical information. They only need to summarize their understanding at the time. Allowing them to revise their notes or drawings adds to their deeper understanding and retention.

Common Mistakes

As with all instructional techniques, there are more and less effective ways to implement. Knowing ahead of time where problems might arise will increase your likelihood of success in implementing this technique. Watch out for these mistakes when you implement the note-taking technique in your classroom:

- The teacher does not directly teach and model for students how to execute the various ways of taking notes.

- The teacher does not allocate enough time for students to process, summarize, and generate their own notes.

- The teacher provides complete notes for students.

- The teacher has students take notes before they have had an opportunity to process and elaborate on the content with their classmates.

- The teacher requires students to take notes while new information is being presented.

- The teacher asks students to record all of the information about a concept rather than teaching them how to differentiate between what is critical content and what is not.

- The teacher requires students to "copy the notes off the board."

Examples and Nonexamples of Note Taking in the Classroom

Following are two sets of examples and nonexamples (one elementary and one secondary) showing how the strategy is implemented in a classroom. While reading these, keep in mind the common mistakes mentioned previously, and note how the example teachers avoid them and the nonexample teachers miss the mark by making one or more of the common mistakes.

Elementary Example of Implementing Note Taking

In this first example, the students are learning about President Lincoln and the Civil War. In addition to a history learning target, this teacher is working toward another learning target: *Determine two or more main ideas of a text and explain how they are supported by key details; summarize the text* (see also CCSS ELA & Literacy, Reading–Informational Text Grade 5).

> Good afternoon, class. Today, we are going to learn about the life of the sixteenth president of the United States, Abraham Lincoln. You are going to learn about President Lincoln in two ways. First, I'm going to tell you some facts, true things about Lincoln's life. Then, you'll watch a video about Lincoln. Your job is to listen carefully and remember the important information from the facts I told you and from the video you watch. As soon as the video ends, you will work with your partner to create a free-flowing web that tells the important information you learned about Abraham Lincoln.

The teacher proceeds to share information and show the video about Abraham Lincoln's life. She briefly reminds them that to create a free-flowing web, they need to draw larger circles to indicate a more important concept and draw smaller circles to indicate supporting information. Working together with a partner, the students determine the important information from the presentation and video and create free-flowing webs to record this information. Figure 2.1 is an example of how a free-flowing web might look for this lesson on Abraham Lincoln.

Figure 2.1: Example of a Free-Flowing Web

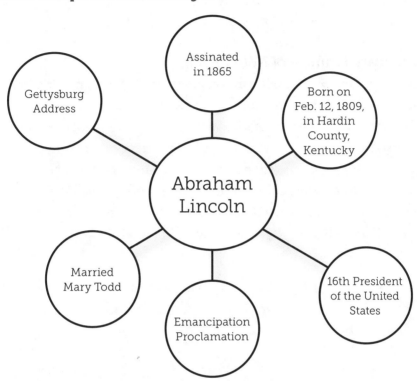

Elementary Nonexample of Taking Notes

Our elementary nonexample is based on the same grade level and learning target as the previous example. This teacher makes one of the most common mistakes in using the technique of note taking. See if you can identify it as you visit her classroom.

> Good afternoon, class. Today, we are going to learn about Abraham Lincoln's life. First, I'm going to give you some important information about our sixteenth president. After that, I will show a short video. After the video, you will work with your partner and create a free-flowing web that includes all the information you learned about Abraham Lincoln.

In this nonexample, the teacher is asking students to record everything they learn regardless of the importance of the information. She neglects to remind students that they must prioritize the importance of the details by placing them in appropriately sized circles. The students' free-flowing webs become unmanageable, and since the teacher does not guide students to analyze and synthesize the critical content, they will have difficulty summarizing what is most important about President Lincoln.

Secondary Example of Note Taking

The secondary example is an introduction of the periodic table of elements to a high school science classroom. The learning target is: *The sub-atomic structural model and interactions between electric charges at the atomic scale can be used to explain the structure and interactions of matter, including chemical reactions and nuclear processes. Repeating patterns of the periodic table reflect patterns of outer electrons. A stable molecule has less energy than the same set of atoms separated; one must provide at least this energy to take the molecule apart* (NGSS Physical Sciences Grades 9–12: Structure of Matter, Nuclear Processes).

In this example, the teacher first presents a chunk of information introducing the periodic table, identifying the critical information students need to know about the table and how to read it.

> Good morning, class. Today, we are going to delve into the fascinating complexities of the periodic table of elements. First, we will focus on the structure of the table and how to understand the different parts. I would like you to create an informal outline with the critical information you would like to remember. Recall, in an informal outline, the most important concepts are written on the far left of your notes, and the supporting concepts are indented. You can begin your outline while I am presenting. However, as usual, after my instruction, I will give you an opportunity to discuss the periodic table in your groups and additional time to work on your outline.

After this brief introduction, the teacher presents a chunk of information about the periodic table. She then gives the students time to discuss (process) with their group what they learned. After the discussion time is over, she gives them some time to create or finish their informal outlines. Figure 2.2 is an example of an informal outline describing the periodic table of the elements.

Figure 2.2: Example of an Informal Outline

Periodic Table of the Elements

I. A group is a vertical column in the periodic table

    A. 18 groups

    B. Some groups contain elements with very similar properties

    C. Number of valence shell electrons determines group

II. A period is a horizontal row in the periodic table

    A. 7 periods

    B. Some periods also show similar properties

    C. Total number of electron shells determines period

III. Elements are listed in order of increasing atomic number

    A. Number of protons in atomic number

(Reprinted by permission from Marzano & Brown, 2009, p. 71)

Secondary Nonexample of Taking Notes

In this nonexample, the teacher begins the lesson the same way. Notice the common mistake he makes.

> Good morning, class. Today, we are going to learn about the periodic table of elements. We will discuss the structure of the table and how to understand the different parts. I am providing you with an informal outline containing the critical information you should know. As usual, after my instruction, I will give you an opportunity to discuss the periodic table in your groups.

After this brief introduction, the teacher hands out the informal outline and presents a chunk of information about the periodic table. He then gives the students time to discuss (process) with their group what they learned.

In this nonexample, the teacher is providing the informal outline to the students rather than giving them an opportunity to generate the outline independently or with a partner. By providing this outline, the teacher deprives the students of the opportunity to analyze and synthesize the information they received and then determine what is critical and what is not.

Determining If Students Can Record and Represent Knowledge Using Note Taking

Monitoring for the desired result is a critical part of using an instructional strategy. The desired result of recording and representing knowledge is that students are able to understand and convey the content in an accurate way. If you have taught your students how to take notes, here are some ways that you can monitor your students' understanding of critical content as a result of their note taking:

- Students turn in notes that demonstrate they understand and have recorded the content accurately.

- Students' notes contain critical information about content.

- Students can explain the main points of the lesson using their notes.

- The exit slips students turn in at the end of class contain the top three critical pieces of information they learned/noted in the day's lesson.

Table 2.1 is a student proficiency scale for note taking that can be used and adapted as necessary to determine how students are progressing in their ability to accurately understand critical information they have recorded in their notes.

Table 2.1: Student Proficiency Scale for Note Taking

Emerging	Fundamental	Desired Result
Students generate notes, but they do not identify the big ideas or details of the lesson.	Students can generate notes that identify the big ideas in the lesson but lack details.	Students can successfully generate notes that identify the big ideas and details in the lesson.
Students generate notes that include all the information, whether it is critical or not.	Students can generate notes including some, but not all, of the big ideas and details in the lesson.	Students can successfully generate notes that summarize the critical information in the lesson without help from a peer partner or the teacher.
Students are unable to generate notes that summarize the critical information in the lesson without help from a peer partner or the teacher.	Students can generate simple summaries in their own words but need support from the teacher.	Students are able to explain the summarization of critical information in their notes to their peers or teacher.

Scaffold and Extend Instruction to Meet Students' Needs

As you become more skilled at showing students how to record and represent knowledge through note taking, you will find that you can more readily identify individuals or small groups of students who need something more or different than the original instruction. Some students need support or scaffolding that takes them from where they are to where they need to be. Other students need to be challenged by the teacher extending the ways in which she expects them to interact with critical content. Teachers can use the following suggestions as springboards for zeroing in on the needs of their students.

Scaffolding

When students are having difficulty identifying central ideas and details as well as writing them down in their notes, try one of the following ways to adjust your instruction:

- Post examples of various resources that students can consult when they need help with note taking. These resources can include 1) student-friendly definitions of the previously described methods of note taking, along with student examples; 2) templates for students who need the extra structure, such as the numbering and indenting for an informal outline; and 3) step-by-step directions in student-friendly language for note taking.

- Provide guided notes with a fill-in-the-blank format in which the teacher has already filled in some of the information. Students are responsible for filling in the answers after having an opportunity to process and elaborate on the critical information from the chunk of information or demonstration the teacher presented.

Extending

For some students, you may need to go beyond what you assigned to the class. Try these ideas for extending the usual tasks of note taking:

- Ask students to prioritize the information they have recorded.

- Ask students to write definitions in their own words of the key vocabulary.

- Ask students to choose one of the big ideas from the lesson that they would like to research further and then develop a preliminary outline of the critical content.

PART II

NONLINGUISTIC REPRESENTATIONS

Nonlinguistic representations depict the critical information of a concept through the use of methods other than language. Graphic and visual representations, dramatic enactments, and mnemonic devices can enhance students' understanding and processing of information, skills, and procedures. When paired with linguistic representations, such as summarizing and note taking, these techniques will provide you with a powerful set of tools to aid students in analyzing and synthesizing content and retaining critical information.

Part II contains four techniques that show you how to teach and model for students how to represent knowledge using nonlinguistic representations:

- Instructional Technique 3: Graphic Organizers

- Instructional Technique 4: Pictorial Notes and Pictographs

- Instructional Technique 5: Dramatic Enactments

- Instructional Technique 6: Mnemonic Devices

Instructional Technique 3

GRAPHIC ORGANIZERS

Graphic organizers are nonlinguistic representations of critical content. Teaching and modeling the purpose of a graphic organizer is a frequently forgotten step when your lesson plans include an organizer. You can all too easily assume that students understand organizers because they are used in every classroom. However, the big idea of using organizers is not how fancy they are or how much time you spend designing them. The big idea is that graphic organizers should enable students to organize new knowledge in ways that make learning more meaningful and memorable. If after the use of a specific organizer your students are not able to summarize and explain the content within, you need to return to the drawing board—not necessarily to develop a new organizer, but evaluate how effectively you have directly instructed and modeled for students how to use the organizer.

Students record their knowledge using nonlinguistic organizers that correspond to specific patterns commonly found in information. Initially, if students are new to this technique, teachers must choose the best graphic organizer to represent the information. Teachers need to instruct how to use a variety of visual tools and graphic organizers. After they have a greater understanding of the purposes of different types of organizers and how to use them, they will eventually be able to identify independently the best organizer for a given assignment.

How to Effectively Implement Graphic Organizers

To effectively implement graphic organizers, you must master the following instructional tasks:

- understand the relationship of summarizing to graphic organizers

- teach all of your students the critical attributes of graphic organizers

- choose graphic organizers that are most appropriate for your grade level and content

- teach all of your students how to use each of the graphic organizers that you intend to work with frequently in your classroom

Understand the Relationship of Summarizing to Graphic Organizers

The genius of graphic organizers lies in the way they can help your students' brains more efficiently process and remember critical content. When students create a one-page visual representation of a process, historical event, or two-hundred-page novel, it reduces the cognitive overload that can occur when the brain is trying to remember too much all at once. After the students record a central idea or key details on an organizer, their minds are free to think about the next step. Graphic organizers very effectively help students execute the steps of summarizing mentioned earlier in the guide. Once students have heard the presentation or read the text, the organizer forces them to think of ways to chunk (divide the information into the parts of the organizer), compact (get rid of trivial information because the organizer doesn't provide enough room for it), and conceptualize (think of words and phrases that best fit what the organizer requires).

Summarizing is a way of recording knowledge that almost always uses just words. Lots of words take up lots of space, both on the page and in the brain of the reader. There is little working memory left to analyze and summarize the text. Organizing by using graphic representations is a unique way of summarizing using many fewer words than one finds in text. Placing key words and phrases into the shapes and designs of flowcharts, diagrams, concept maps, and hundreds of other types of organizers gives students new ways to learn and retain critical content. When you begin to teach students how to use or perhaps eventually design their own organizers in the upper grades, remember that organizing is just another way of summarizing. In fact, organizers can serve as an ideal scaffold for students who experience difficulties with summarizing.

Teach Your Students the Critical Attributes of Graphic Organizers

Following are the critical attributes of graphic organizers:

- Graphic organizers are designed to communicate information about certain disciplines and certain types of text structures. Specific types of organizers are designed for use with specific kinds of text. Imagine attempting to complete a compare/contrast organizer from text in which the author does no comparing whatsoever.

- Graphic organizers have what are called text frames. These are questions, categories, terms, or concepts that communicate to students what type of information they should write in or on the geometric shapes, lines, and arrows. Consider what one of your favorite organizers would look like absent its text frames. The text frames bring the organizer to life and dictate to students exactly what they should be looking for as they listen to a lesson presentation or read a text. Essential to completing a graphic organizer accurately is a solid understanding of the specialized terms.

- Some graphic organizers are quite well known and associated with the individuals who developed them. One example is the Frayer Model (see Resource A.9) developed by a University of Wisconsin professor to build vocabulary among her students. You and your students can design your own organizers, but take care to determine what the text frames will say, what categories of information will be placed in the frames, and what kind of questions the organizer will answer.

- Organizers use a wide variety of specialized academic terms. You can assume that your students know precisely what they mean, especially if they are older. However, here are some of the academic terms found as text frames in any collection of organizers: *synonyms, antonyms, fact, topic, concept, main idea, detail, central idea, critical information, circumstances, consequences, cause, effect, similarities, differences,* and many, many more. The enormous benefits of using graphic organizers can quickly vanish if students don't have a solid understanding of what the labels for the text frames mean and what questions the organizer is designed to answer about new content.

- Organizers are very valuable learning tools for students, who can carry them through grade levels and into their careers or college. However, you may need to convince students about the value of mastering the technique over time so they will be ready to assume the responsibility for selecting their own organizers and become more capable organizers of their own learning.

Table 3.1 is a brief lesson introducing students to the generic concept of organizers. This lesson assumes very little prior experience using graphic organizers and would be suitable for lower-grade students or upper-grade students who may be struggling readers.

Table 3.1: A Lesson Plan for Graphic Organizers

Step	Discussion
Project several simple graphic organizers (without the usual frames) on your SMART Board or screen. Show organizers that you know you will likely use with your students.	Ask students to look at the blank and frameless organizers and ask them, "Can anyone tell me what these are?" Some students may guess that they are part of a math class. Others might think you plan to show them how to draw animals using geometric shapes. Hopefully, you have one or two students who recognize the figures and can name them as organizers or graphic organizers.
Give students a student-friendly definition of the term *graphic organizer.*	A graphic organizer is a visual illustration of a verbal statement. In other words, an organizer is a picture illustrating something that was written or spoken. You may work with this definition until it flows for you and your students. They need to understand that the purpose of making organizers is to translate lots of words into one simple picture with just a few words.
Ask students, "Have you noticed anything about the organizers up on the board?"	Hopefully, someone will recognize that these organizers have no text frames. There are no clues as to what students should write in the various spots of the organizer.
Change the slide to the one that has the previous organizers displayed with their text frames.	At this point in the lesson, point out to students that when they fill out an organizer, they must know the meanings of all of the words (text frames). If they do not understand the words, they will not be able to complete the organizer. In the instances of prereaders, who may not yet be able to fluently read the text, be sure to explain and show examples of the information that needs to be drawn or written on the organizer.
On the next slide, project completed organizers showing students how their organizers will look at some point.	For prereaders, develop a sample organizer that contains pictures that students will readily recognize. For example, use an organizer that has four large rectangles with the following labels written underneath: *Main Character, Setting, Problem,* and *Solution.* Draw pictures that tell a story you have recently read aloud so students can see how they might complete such an organizer with their own drawings. For older students, use a story-board organizer in which students illustrate various scenes or sections from a novel. For example, using the novel *Hatchet* by Gary Paulsen, teachers can find pictures that illustrate the five big scenes in the story: airplane ride, crash in the lake, survival in the wilderness Part I, survival in the wilderness part II, and rescue.

Step	Discussion
In conclusion, ask students to use one of the organizers to visualize a story you have read aloud or a novel students are reading as part of a language arts class.	This lesson plan has focused on narrative text, but the principles apply to whatever content or organizers you plan to use with students. Always conclude any lesson that includes a graphic organizer by asking students to write a short summary using the information from their organizer.

Choose Graphic Organizers That Are Most Appropriate for Your Grade Level and Content

As you consider which organizers are most appropriate for your grade level and content, use the following tables as guides. Table 3.2 describes some of the most common organizers in more detail and points you to where they can be found in this guide—either in Resource A or in the classroom examples.

Table 3.2: Common Graphic Organizers

Title of Organizer	Description
Analogy Chart	Use this organizer to connect new learning to familiar concepts. For example, compare cells as the building blocks of the human body to bricks and lumber as the building blocks of a house. See a template in Resource A.4.
Cause/Effect Organizer	Use this organizer for identifying and analyzing the cause(s) and effect(s) of an event or process. See a template in Resource A.5.
Column Organizer	Use this organizer to classify information into groups. The number of columns used depends on the classifications being made. See a template in Resource A.6.
Concept Map	Use concept maps to take notes during presentations, to guide reading assignments, as a study guide for test preparation, as a tool to assist in writing a summary of the text, or as an ongoing summarizing and review of concepts discussed during each class period. In a concept map, students identify key concepts and join them with connecting words showing the nature of their relationship. See a sample concept map in Figure 3.1.
Descriptive Organizer	Use this organizer to represent facts about specific persons, places, things, and events. See a template in Resource A.7.

(continued on next page)

Table 3.2 *(continued)*

Title of Organizer	Description
Episode Organizer	Use this organizer to record information about specific events (e.g., a historic event, like the invasion of Normandy). See a template in Resource A.8.
Frayer Model	Use this organizer to elaborate and expand a specific word or term. Aspects of the organizer include 1) definition of a word, 2) facts or characteristics of the word, and 3) examples/nonexamples of the word. See a template in Resource A.9.
Generalization Organizer	Use this organizer to compare pieces of evidence to see what they have in common and then make a statement that is true based on that evidence. See a template in Resource A.10.
Simple Story Map	Use this organizer to help map out the beginning, middle, and end of a story. See a simple story map template in Resource A.11.
Time Sequence/Sequence Chain/Chain of Events Organizers	Use these organizers for topics that involve a linear chain of events, with a definite beginning, middle, and end. See a time sequence template in Resource A.12.
Vocabulary Web	Use this organizer to elaborate on the meaning of key vocabulary essential to understanding new content. See a vocabulary web template in Resource A.13 and a completed vocabulary web in Figure 3.2.

Table 3.3 lists organizers by text types, or in the case of mathematics, organizers appropriate for specialized content. Choose an organizer that is best suited for teaching your content. The organizer needs to fit the type of text, whether expository or narrative, as well as the text structure the author uses. If the critical content is presented in a historical sequence, then a time-line is appropriate. If the text compares several geographical locations, then a compare/contrast organizer is the best choice. Choosing the wrong organizer for the text or presentation you are teaching will likely negate any positive effects on learning. If you want to find additional information about the organizers in Table 3.3, use your favorite search engine and plug in the organizer's name.

Table 3.3: Organizers Listed by Text Type/Content

Organizers for Nonfiction (Expository Text)	Organizers for Fiction (Narrative Text)	Organizers for Mathematics
Analogy	Cause/effect	Chart
Cause/effect	Concept map	Concept map
Chain of command	Matrix	Diagram
Chain of events	Network tree	Equation
Chart	Picture	Image
Compare/contrast matrix	Problem/solution outline	Matrix
Concept map	Puzzle	Picture
Continuum scale	Relay summary	Semantic features analysis
Crossword puzzle	Semantic features analysis	Semantic word map
Cycle	Semantic word map	
Diagram	Series of events chain	
Entailment mesh	Spider map	
Fishbone diagram	Story frame	
Flowchart	Story grammar	
Frayer model	Story map	
Grid	Talking drawings	
Hierarchy	Timeline	
Historical figure character map	Venn diagram	
Human-interaction outline	Web	
Life-cycle phases	Why/because pursuit chart	
Network tree		
Semantic features analysis		
Semantic word map		
Spider map		
Timeline		

(Reprinted by permission from McEwan, 2007.)

Common Mistakes

Given the diversity of your students and the complexity of the critical content you are expected to teach, mistakes in implementation are almost inevitable. However, knowing in advance about possible pitfalls can help you avoid them. Here are some common mistakes that can occur when you are trying to help your students learn how to use graphic organizers to represent content knowledge:

- The teacher does not teach students how to use a graphic organizer.

- The teacher does not provide enough time for students to process content, summarize it, and complete a graphic organizer.

- The teacher provides completed graphic organizers for students.

- The teacher requires students to complete a graphic organizer during the introduction of a chunk of new information instead of giving them time to process and elaborate before creating the organizer.

- The teacher asks students to include all the information about a concept in a graphic organizer rather than differentiate between what is critical and what is not.

- The teacher provides an inappropriate graphic-organizer format for the type of information to be learned.

Examples and Nonexamples of Using Graphic Organizers

Following are two sets of examples and corresponding nonexamples (one elementary and one secondary) of how the graphic-organizers technique can be used in a classroom. As you are reading the examples, keep in mind the mistakes that you can make while implementing this strategy, and consider how a teacher might monitor for the desired result of recording and representing knowledge in each example.

Elementary Example of Graphic Organizers

In this first example, fifth-grade students are learning about states of matter. The learning target is: *Matter of any type can be subdivided into particles that are too small to see, but even then the matter still exists and can be detected by other means. A model showing that gases are made from matter particles that are too small to see and are moving freely around in space can explain many observations, including the inflation and shape of a balloon and the effects of air on larger particles or objects* (NGSS Physical Sciences Grade 5: Structure and Properties of Matter).

> Good morning, class. Today, we are going to learn about the states of matter. First, we'll watch a video that describes the different states of matter. Then, you'll discuss in your small groups what you learned from the video. For your recording activity today, we are going to learn how to create a concept map. Concept maps are different from many of the organizers we have used. Concept maps require you not only to identify critical concepts but also to show how the various concepts on the map are related to each other by writing connecting words on the lines of the organizer. I'm going to show you a very simple concept map that I created using computer software. If you love all kinds of reptiles, you've probably read dozens of books about them. You will be very familiar with the concepts, and you can see how the various concepts about reptiles are related to each other. Notice that the connecting words you choose have to form a simple sentence that describes the relationship between the two concepts. *The teacher puts Figure 3.1 on the screen (see page 52).*

The teacher shows the video about the states of matter. Then the class divides up into small groups for discussion about the important points the students identified in the video. The teacher follows the small group discussions with a whole group discussion to facilitate elaboration on the critical concepts. The teacher creates the concept map on a large bulletin board, and students will work on the connecting words in tomorrow's class.

Elementary Nonexample of Graphic Organizers

Our elementary nonexample is based on the same grade level and learning target as our elementary example. However, this teacher is making one of the most common errors in using the technique of graphic organizers to

Figure 3.1: Concept Map Example

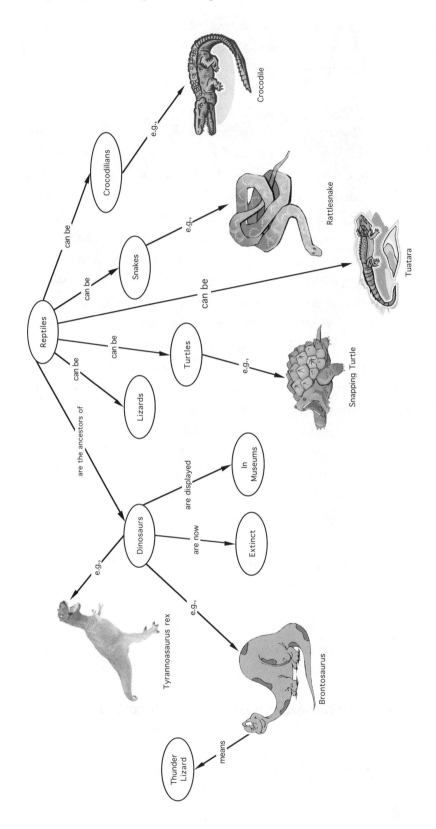

represent content knowledge—failing to teach and model how to create an organizer for her students.

The teacher begins with the same introduction, and the class watches the video. Instead of small group discussions or a large group discussion, the teacher has the students immediately complete the concept map. In this non-example, the teacher is asking students to represent their understanding of the concept without the benefit of processing through small group discussions or elaborating during the large group discussion.

Secondary Example of Graphic Organizers

The secondary example is a lesson on determining the meaning of words in informational text. The learning target is: *Determine the meaning of words and phrases as they are used in a text, including figurative, connotative, and technical meanings* (see also CCSS ELA & Literacy, Reading–Informational Text Grade 6).

Good morning, class. One of the most challenging things you face every day in school is learning all of the new vocabulary in this class. Sometimes you can memorize definitions of words from the glossary, but all too often after you've memorized the definition, you still don't really understand the word. Today, we are going to chorally partner read a section from our science text. As you read, I want you to be looking for our new word of the day: *transformation*. Pay special attention to where in the reading this new word pops up. Notice if the word is defined anywhere and if the text gives you any special information about this word. When we finish reading the passage, I would like you to complete a vocabulary web for one of the terms we discussed. I will be handing out a template for you to use for this web.

Figure 3.2 is an example of what the vocabulary web might look like using the word *transformation*.

Figure 3.2: Vocabulary Web for the *Word Transformation*

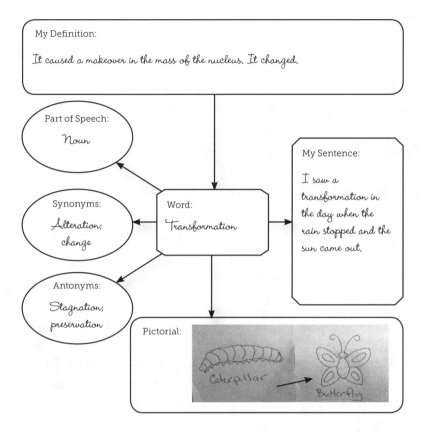

Secondary Nonexample of Graphic Organizers

In this nonexample, the teacher begins her lesson the same way as the teacher in the example. Please note where the teacher makes an error that prevents students from getting the cognitive and retention benefits from completing the graphic organizer.

> Good morning, class. Today, we are going to chorally read our science text together. I will stop during the reading to discuss terms that may be new for the class. If you hear a word you are uncertain about, please write it on your whiteboard to get my attention. When we finish reading the passage, I would like you to study the completed vocabulary web for one of the terms we discuss—*transformation*. I will be handing out the completed vocabulary web.

In this nonexample, the teacher provides the completed vocabulary web shown in Figure 3.2 to her students rather than giving them the opportunity to complete the web themselves. By doing this, the teacher does not give the students a chance to analyze and synthesize the information for themselves.

Determining If Students Can Represent Knowledge Using Graphic Organizers

There are multiple ways for you to monitor your students while they are recording critical content on their graphic organizers, including the following:

- Ask students to participate in a think-pair-share. The "think" is the completion of the graphic organizer. Students are "paired" with other students, and they "share" their graphic organizers. The teacher monitors by circulating around the room and listening to the conversations of each pair to determine if the students have captured the important information.

- Ask students to attach their completed graphic organizer to their academic notebook, and check each academic notebook after the lesson.

- Ask students to complete A–Z sentence summaries. At the end of instruction or after reading, the students are assigned a letter from the alphabet and asked to create a one-sentence summary of the instruction or reading that begins with their assigned letter. Students can share their one-sentence summaries with peers in a pair-share, chalkboard splash (students post their work in an assigned spot on the whiteboard or bulletin board), and so on.

Table 3.4 displays a student proficiency scale for graphic organizers. Teachers can use and adapt as necessary to determine how their students are progressing in their ability to accurately encode critical information.

Table 3.4: Student Proficiency Scale for Graphic Organizers

Emerging	Fundamental	Desired Result
Students complete a graphic organizer, but they do not identify the big ideas or details of the lesson. Students complete a graphic organizer that includes all the information, whether it is critical or not. Students are unable to complete a graphic organizer that summarizes the critical information in the lesson without help from a peer partner or the teacher.	Students can complete a graphic organizer that identifies the big ideas but not the supporting details of the lesson. Students can complete a graphic organizer including some of the big ideas and details but cannot explain the relationships as shown by their graphic organizer.	Students can successfully complete a graphic organizer that accurately represents the big ideas and details in the lesson. Students are able to explain the relationships as shown by their graphic organizer to their peers/teacher.

Scaffold and Extend Instruction to Meet Students' Needs

Getting to know your students and planning ahead of time for how to meet their needs will be helpful. Often, the supports and extensions designed to help individual students can be used class-wide to the benefit of all students.

Scaffolding

- Provide examples on the bulletin board or classroom walls of completed graphic organizers.

- Create a display that shows different types of graphic organizers and explains their purposes.

- Pair struggling students with stronger peers so they can complete their organizers together.

Extending

- Have students create their own graphic-organizer format for specific patterns or types of information. This can be used only if the student has a firm grasp of the purpose of graphic organizers, along with the concept being learned.

Instructional Technique 4

PICTORIAL NOTES AND PICTOGRAPHS

Every teacher has heard the timeworn phrase, "A picture is worth a thousand words." Perhaps the visuals your students create to represent information will not portray the essence of a thousand words, but they are most definitely an important way to represent certain kinds of information. There are many ways to represent content in visual ways, including photographs, drawings, paintings, and other types of fine art. However, the two most powerful and easy-to-use visual approaches to represent critical content are pictorial notes and pictographs. Pictorial notes often serve as illustrations for written notes. However, pictorial notes can stand alone if they sufficiently represent the critical content, such as a quickly drawn diagram of a scientific process or a scene from a literary work.

Pictographs come in two formats. The first format is a visual representation of statistical data in the form of a "picture graph." A pictograph showing several small boxes containing multiple photos/illustrations of an object quickly communicates the message of the "what" (i.e., automobiles or apples or kindergarten-age children) and the "how many" more memorably than either a verbal statement or a mathematical graph or chart. In instances where very large quantities are being pictured, include a simple footnote explaining that each picture is worth a thousand or ten thousand units of the specific object.

Pictographs can also be symbols belonging to a pictorial graphic system such as the system of symbols developed by the Department of Transportation to represent locations on the highways and in public places. These pictorial graphics can be read and understood irrespective of an individual's ability to understand English. More recently, pictographs have come to be associated with drawn stick figures, very simple sketches of a person or animal, curves, and dots similar to the pictographs found on the walls of ancient caves. No special artistic talent is required to draw simple pictographs. The benefits of using pictorial notes are that all students know what it means to draw a picture (although artistic abilities will differ), and representing knowledge with an original drawing allows students some flexibility in communicating what their mental image of a given concept might be. Viewing a pictograph can also give you a very immediate idea of the level of understanding a student has for a specific concept.

How to Effectively Implement Pictorial Notes and Pictographs

One method for effectively implementing pictorial notes is to have students draw and share a picture with a partner after each chunk of information within a lesson. At the end of the lesson, the teacher asks the students to draw one picture that consolidates what they have learned in the lesson. It is helpful to have the students write a summary sentence below the picture, too. They can draw the pictures on a specific template or in their academic notebooks.

Pictographs often are used in math or science (and the examples are abundant in these content areas), but you can also use them in other content areas. In a pictograph, students use symbols to represent big ideas or critical information. A pictograph can be used to show the sequence of events in a story. Figure 4.1 is a simplified example of how a student might show the sequence of events for a character in a story.

Figure 4.1: Example of Pictograph

Common Mistakes

Many teachers have experienced the sinking feeling that comes from getting off on the wrong foot during a lesson. Here are some common mistakes to avoid when using pictorial notes and pictographs in your classroom:

- The teacher does not provide enough or even any time for students to process, summarize, and draw a pictorial note or construct a pictograph.

- The teacher requires students to complete pictorial notes and pictographs while a chunk of new information is being presented instead of giving them time to process and elaborate first.

- The teacher provides completed pictorial notes or pictographs for all students.

- The teacher asks students to include all the information about a concept in a pictorial note or pictograph rather than differentiate between what is critical and what is not.

- The teacher puts undue emphasis on students' artistic skills and the quality of students' drawings.

Examples and Nonexamples of Using Pictorial Notes and Pictographs in the Classroom

Following are two sets of examples and nonexamples (one elementary and one secondary) of how the technique of pictorial notes and pictographs can be used in classrooms. Remember to consider how the teachers might monitor for the desired result of recording and representing knowledge in each example.

Elementary Example of Using Pictorial Notes and Pictographs

In this example, the learning target is: *Use addition and subtraction within 20 to solve word problems involving situations of adding to, taking from, putting together, taking apart, and comparing, with unknowns in all positions, e.g., by using objects, drawings, and equations with a symbol for the unknown number to represent the problem* (CCSS for Mathematics for Grade 1).

Good morning, class. Today, we are going to learn how to solve word problems. We will be using pictographs to help us see exactly what the word problem is asking us to do. The handout I have given you is a template to help you create a pictograph. In a pictograph, you use pictures to represent information in the word problem so that it is easier to solve. We will work on the first word problem together. The word problem tells us there were four boxes of blueberries sold in January, nine boxes sold in February, five boxes sold in March, and two boxes sold in April. The question we must answer is this: How many boxes of blueberries were sold altogether in the first four months of the year? We're going to create a pictograph to help us figure out the answer. Here's an example so you can see how I am using the pictograph to represent the boxes of blueberries being sold each month. In my pictograph, I am going to draw four boxes of blueberries in the first row *(see Table 4.1)*.

Table 4.1 Pictograph Example: Number of Boxes of Blueberries Sold Each Month

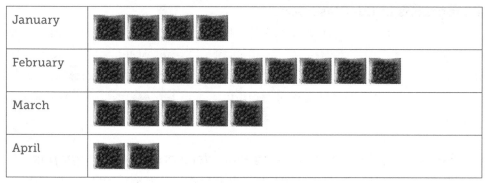

January	
February	
March	
April	

After the teacher completes the first row with students, she asks them to help her complete the second row of the pictograph to show how many boxes of blueberries were sold during February. She then asks them to work with their partners to complete their pictographs for the rows of March and April. Next, she asks them to answer several questions using the information in their pictograph: 1) How many boxes of blueberries were sold altogether? 2) During which month were the most blueberries sold? 3) In which month were the fewest blueberries sold?

Elementary Nonexample of Pictorial Notes and Pictographs

This nonexample uses the same lesson as above. Look for the error in the teacher's implementation of this strategy.

> Good morning, class. Today, we are going to begin learning how to solve word problems. We will be using pictographs to help us see what the word problem is asking us to do. The handout I have given you is a template to use to help you create a pictograph. In a pictograph, you use pictures to represent the information in the word problem so that it is easier to solve. The word problem says there were four boxes of blueberries sold in January. I would like you to draw four boxes of blueberries in the first row of your pictograph to represent the four boxes of blueberries sold in January, and then complete the rest of the rows in your pictograph so you can figure out the total number of boxes of blueberries that were sold.

In this nonexample, the teacher did not directly teach or model for her students how to use a pictograph to represent the total number of boxes of blueberries that were sold. She may get many different interpretations or representations based on each student's understanding of the pictograph concept and may lose the benefit of using the pictograph to display and interpret word problems, which was the goal of the lesson.

Secondary Example of Pictorial Notes and Pictographs

In our secondary example, a high school science class is beginning a study of the circulatory system. The learning target is: *Develop and use a model to illustrate the hierarchical organization of interacting systems that provide specific functions within multicellular organisms* (NGSS Grades 9–12: From Molecules to Organisms).

Good afternoon, class. Today, we are going to continue our study of the circulatory system. I assigned the first section of the chapter as reading homework and asked you to jot down some key words and ideas before you came to class. Now, I would like you to reread that section of your textbook. During your rereading of the information or right after you finish, I would like you to create a pictorial note to represent the critical information about the circulatory system that you learned from the text. Below your pictorial note, please add a summary statement. I will give you the next thirty minutes to complete the reading and picture. After the thirty minutes, you will have time to meet with your group and share your pictures. You may add additional information to your pictorial notes or make changes if you feel you need to do so after sharing with each other.

In this example, the teacher gives an appropriate amount of time for his students to create their pictorial notes and is able to monitor for the desired result by walking around the room and speaking with the students individually. Figure 4.2 is an example of what a student's pictorial notes might look like for this example.

Figure 4.2: Pictorial Notes Representing the Circulatory System

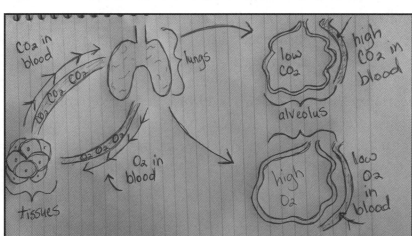

Secondary Nonexample of Pictorial Notes and Pictographs

The nonexample uses the same lesson and pictorial notes but has one critical difference: the teacher has instructed the students that points will be taken off for sloppy or poorly drawn notes. The purpose of pictorial notes or pictographs is not how neat or well drawn they are but how well they represent the learning—the big ideas and supporting details.

Determining If Students Can Represent Critical Content Using Pictorial Notes or Pictographs

Following are some ways to monitor whether your students are achieving the desired effect:

- Walk around the room to check whether students' pictorial notes or pictographs represent critical content.

- Collect the pictorial notes or pictographs and check whether the students represented the critical information accurately. Although this work might not be graded, it could include some feedback about critical content that may have been missed.

- Ask your students to post their pictorial notes or pictographs on an assigned spot on the whiteboard or bulletin board.

- Conduct a group discussion to discover what students learned from this process about the critical content.

Use the student proficiency scale for pictorial notes and pictographs (Table 4.2) to determine how well your students are progressing in their abilities to represent critical content using either pictorial notes or pictographs.

Table 4.2: Student Proficiency Scale for Pictorial Notes or Pictographs

Emerging	Fundamental	Desired Result
Students create pictorial notes or pictographs, but the students do not identify the big ideas or details of the lesson.	Students can create pictorial notes/pictographs that identify the big ideas but not the supporting details of the lesson.	Students can successfully create pictorial notes or pictographs that accurately represent the big ideas and details in the lesson.
Students create pictorial notes/pictographs that include all the information, whether it is critical or not.	Students can create pictorial notes/pictographs that include some of the big ideas and details in the lesson.	Students are able to explain their pictorial notes or pictographs to their peers or the teacher in a summarizing statement.
Students are unable to create pictorial notes or pictographs that summarize the critical information in the lesson without help from a peer partner or the teacher.		

Scaffold and Extend Instruction to Meet Students' Needs

When you plan ahead for scaffolding and extending instruction, you are more likely to adapt the instruction for students' needs during a lesson. Here are some ways to scaffold and extend instruction to help your students understand the primary goal of representing knowledge by using pictorial notes or pictographs. The process will enable them to understand and remember critical content.

Scaffolding

- Post student-created pictorial notes or pictographs that struggling students can use as benchmark examples against which to measure their own work.

- If students are having a difficult time determining which information to represent through their pictorial notes or pictographs, meet with them individually or in a small group to provide the additional support.

- For students who have difficulty creating visual representation, provide them with graphic images from computer software. These can be cut out and available for them to attach to their paper. A teacher will need to have a large selection of graphics so students can be creative with their representations.

Extending

- Use more advanced software to create more professional-looking representations of critical information, which can possibly include animation.

- Assign the creators of the advanced representations to make presentations to small groups or the entire class.

Instructional Technique 5

DRAMATIC ENACTMENTS

With dramatic enactments, students roleplay characters or act out scenes, processes, or events. Students may also act out or symbolize key content. Dramatic enactments are engaging, motivating, and aid in retention. When students act out the content during a critical-input experience, the likelihood they will retain the information is heightened. The greatest benefits come when students are required to explain the connections between the dramatic enactment and the key content.

How to Effectively Implement Dramatic Enactment

There are different ways to use dramatic enactment, from presenting a readers' theater to roleplaying a process. To effectively implement this strategy so that students achieve the desired result, you should have an organized and well-thought-out plan for keeping students focused and develop specific rules and procedures to manage the activity. For example, each student should have a defined role or responsibility in the dramatic enactment. Here are descriptions of some ways teachers can use dramatic enactment in the classroom:

- *Readers' Theater:* Readers' theater is a dramatic presentation of a written work. Students read from a "script," and reading parts are divided among the students. No memorization, costumes, blocking, or special lighting is required or needed. The focus of readers' theater is on reading the text with expressive voices and gestures so that the comprehension of text becomes meaningful, memorable, and enjoyable for students. For readers' theater to be effective and successful, it is important that teachers give students enough time to read through and practice a script. For example, a teacher might give the script to students on a Monday and hold the performance on a Friday. Sample scripts are readily available on the Internet.

- *Role Play:* In a role-playing activity, students learn kinesthetically by acting out the parts of a concept or process. This encourages students to think about their connections to the concept or process. Teachers begin with a discussion that leads to a brief introduction or chunk of information. Then they give students time to process and elaborate individually or in groups.

  At the time of this guide's publication, an example of a science role play can be found at www.berkshiremuseum.org/living_landscapes/pdf/Berkshire_L6.pdf. The process in this example is the water cycle. Students are assigned roles, such as clouds, trees, ground, streams, lakes, oceans, and water droplets, for the activity. Then the students play their roles as they pertain to the water cycle.

- *Simulation:* A classroom simulation is designed to replicate a real-life situation closely and has students assume roles as they analyze data, make decisions, and solve the problems inherent in the situation. As the simulation proceeds, students respond to the changes within the situation by studying the consequences of their decisions and subsequent actions and then predicting future problems and/or solutions. During the simulation, students perform tasks that enable them to learn. As with the other techniques for recording and representing knowledge, teachers should give students an opportunity to process and elaborate on a new concept before engaging in a simulation.

  Simulations can also be considered processing activities. For the simulation to be considered recording and representing knowledge, it should include time for reflection and recording that allows students to share their experiences. For example, in a simulation called Feudal M&M's, the teacher has students act out different assigned roles, such as king, noble, vassal, and peasant, to enable them to identify the order of societal rank and loyalties within feudal Europe. Students use M&M's to represent the currency they pay for protection, taxes, and so forth.

Common Mistakes

As one of the more unique ways to represent critical content, implementing dramatic enactments comes with its share of common mistakes. These are just a few:

- The teacher does not instruct students how to enact or act out a concept.

- The teacher requires students to create or act out a dramatic enactment after presenting a chunk of new information without giving them time to process and elaborate on the concept first.

- The teacher does not provide any or enough time for students to create or read through and practice a dramatic enactment.

- The teacher asks students to include all the information about a concept in a dramatic enactment rather than differentiate between what is critical and what is not.

- The teacher does not develop specific rules and procedures for the activity.

- The teacher does not have students summarize their learning in some way after the dramatic enactment.

Examples and Nonexamples of Dramatic Enactments in the Classroom

Two examples and nonexamples of dramatic enactments are readers' theater for elementary students and a simulation for high school juniors. Consider what a teacher might do to monitor for the desired result of recording and representing knowledge in each example and nonexample.

Elementary Example of Dramatic Enactment

In this example, second-grade students are learning about fables and folktales. The goal is to have students be able to summarize in their own words the central message or moral of the story. The learning target is: *Recount stories, including fables and folktales from diverse cultures, and determine their central message, lesson, or moral* (see also CCSS ELA & Literacy, Reading–

Literature Grade 2). The students read a tale by Rudyard Kipling called *How the Camel Got His Hump*, a suggested text exemplar for Grades 2–3.

The teacher has decided to use readers' theater for reading and understanding this tale. In preparation, she makes copies of the story for the students to use as scripts. On Monday, she hands out the scripts, explains the activity, and lets them know they will perform this tale on Friday. She reminds them that they do not need to memorize the script and that they should focus on reading the text with expressive voices and gestures. During the week, she gives them some time to practice reading the script. On Friday, the students perform the tale and have a large group discussion about the central idea of the story. At the end of class, the students complete an exit slip with a summary of the central idea in their own words.

Elementary Nonexample of Dramatic Enactment

This nonexample uses the same learning target and text. The teacher does the same preparation ahead of time. After she presents the lesson to the class, she tells the students that they will have thirty minutes to read through and practice the script. When the thirty minutes is over, they will perform the script and have a discussion about the central idea.

Although this activity may have some moderate success, it does not give the students the time to become familiar enough with the script to practice expression and gestures. Their attention during the performance will likely be more focused on reading the right part and not so much on comprehension of the story. Successful implementation would include a few days to become familiar with the tale and comfortable about performing it.

Secondary Example of Dramatic Enactment

This example of simulation will use a slightly different approach. An eleventh-grade social-studies teacher is teaching students about what it was like to be a farmer in the Gilded Age. This fits within the theme of *human beings create, learn, share, and adapt to culture* from the 2014 National Curriculum Standards for Social Studies: Chapter 2—The Themes of Social Studies: *The study of culture examines the socially transmitted beliefs, values, institutions, behaviors, traditions, and way of life of a group of people; it also encompasses other cultural attributes and products, such as language, literature, music, arts and artifacts, and foods* (National Council for the Social Studies, 2014).

In this example, the teacher stops at critical points to have the students discuss the implications of what has happened so far as well as how they feel about them. During these stopping points, students record critical information using a combination-notes format. At the end of class, the teacher ties it all together using a large group discussion to sum up the critical information. Then she has the students write a sentence about one way the Gilded Age is similar to life today and a second sentence that explains how life was different from their experiences today.

Secondary Nonexample of Dramatic Enactment

Using the same lesson as the secondary example, the teacher has the students participate in the same simulation. In this case, the teacher does not stop the students during the simulation and fails to have a discussion at the end of the lesson. Without this discussion, some students may not make the connection between the game-like atmosphere of the simulation and the critical information it represents. The teacher misses opportunities to have students continue to elaborate on a critical concept and expand their understanding and retention.

Determining If Students Can Demonstrate Their Understanding of Content from a Dramatic Enactment

You can be certain that a dramatic enactment has achieved the desired result only if your students are able to both record (through note taking and summarizing) and accurately represent (reenact) the central ideas and key details of the critical content.

There are multiple ways to monitor for the desired result of dramatic enactments, including:

- Ensure that all students participate in a summing-up discussion either by calling on all students or using response chaining. In response chaining, one student elaborates on or clarifies the ideas of another student's answer. This ensures that the teacher is monitoring all students, not just some or the majority.

- Require that students complete an exit slip that summarizes the critical information from the lesson. The students turn those in at the end of class, and the teacher reads through them. If there are students who have not understood the main points of the lesson, the teacher plans to scaffold further learning opportunities for those students during the next class period.

Use the student proficiency scale (Table 5.1) to determine your students' progress toward achieving the desired result with dramatic enactment.

Table 5.1: Student Proficiency Scale for Dramatic Enactment

Emerging	Fundamental	Desired Result
Students can create and participate in a dramatic enactment but cannot identify the big ideas or details of the lesson. Students can create and participate in a dramatic enactment but cannot summarize the critical information in the lesson without help from a peer partner or the teacher.	Students can create and participate in a dramatic enactment and identify the big ideas but not the supporting details of the lesson. Students can create and participate in a dramatic enactment and identify some of the big ideas and details in the lesson, but they cannot produce a short written summary of their understandings.	Students can successfully create and participate in a dramatic enactment and also accurately identify the big ideas and details in the lesson. Students are able to produce a short summary of their learning and explain to their peers and/or teacher how the dramatic enactment helped them summarize the critical information.

Scaffold and Extend Instruction to Meet Students' Needs

The ways in which you scaffold or extend this technique will vary depending on your priorities when you designed the dramatic enactment. Students who are having difficulties reading grade-level text, taking notes, and summarizing will likely find this technique more challenging. On the other hand, there are students whose talents will shine in terms of script writing and acting and with just a bit of scaffolding, they can produce a very accurate oral summary of the information they acquired. Doing the research required to write a brief script for the enactment is a perfect assignment for students whose abilities need a challenging assignment.

Scaffolding

Here are some ways to provide scaffolding for the dramatic enactment technique:

- Ask for student volunteers to participate in the dramatic enactments as models for the whole class before asking the rest of the class to participate. This helps students visualize the expectations of the activity and what it should look like, making them more comfortable with their roles and the responsibility for their parts.

- Pair students to assume the same role. This allows them to help and learn from each other. To monitor for the desired result, teachers can still have them individually summarize the critical input in their own words.

- Provide prompts or a graphic organizer to help students take the notes required to produce a summary after the enactment.

Extending

For those students who need a greater challenge with dramatic enactments, use these extending activities:

- Recruit volunteers to perform as models of the dramatic enactment for the rest of the class.

- Assign one or more students the responsibility for doing more of the research and/or script writing.

- Have students choose a scene or event in the dramatic enactment they felt was critical to representing the concept and explain why they chose that scene or event.

Instructional Technique 6

MNEMONIC DEVICES

Mnemonic devices help students retain and recall pieces of information, such as characteristics, steps, stages, parts, phases, and so forth. A mnemonic-device technique that links to visual imagery—like having a symbol or substitute represent a concept—is the strongest memory tool, and students can use this to remember abstract information. A symbol is something that suggests or reminds the student of the information he is trying to remember (e.g., If your name were Carol Campbell, you might introduce yourself providing two symbols, each standing for a part of the name: "Hi, my name is Carol Campbell. Think Christmas Carol and Campbell's Soup). A substitute is a word that is easy to picture and sounds like the concept.

How to Effectively Implement Mnemonic Devices

As with the other techniques in this guide, teachers should use mnemonic devices only after students have thoroughly processed critical information. In addition, you will need to tell students the meanings of symbols and substitutes as well as how to use them in mnemonic devices. After talking about mnemonic devices, an introductory activity such as the one found in Resource A.14 is one way for you to help students hone their skills in using the different types of mnemonic devices.

There are many types of mnemonic devices, including the following:

Name Mnemonic
Students create a name out of the first letter of each item on a list. You may remember learning about the colors in the spectrum with the name ROY G. BIV (Red, Orange, Yellow, Green, Blue, Indigo, and Violet).

Expression or Word Mnemonic
Students create a sentence or expression that uses the first letter of each item on the list as the first letter of each word in the sentence or expression.

An example of this is the word mnemonic Please Excuse My Dear Aunt Sally for the order of operations in math: Parentheses, Exponents, Multiply, Divide, Add, and Subtract.

Rhyme Mnemonic

Students create a rhyme that helps them remember the information, such as this common one for the number of days in each month:

> *Thirty days hath September,*
>
> *April, June, and November.*
>
> *All the rest have thirty-one;*
>
> *Excepting February alone,*
>
> *Which hath but twenty-eight, in fine,*
>
> *Till leap year gives it twenty-nine.*

Students use this type of mnemonic specifically to remember lists of information or facts. Students create concrete images or pegwords that rhyme with the numbers one through ten. These pegwords are substituted for the number and then associated with key words. An example from *Becoming a Reflective Teacher* (Marzano, 2012a) is:

One is a bun	*Six is a stack of sticks*
Two is a shoe	*Seven is heaven*
Three is a tree	*Eight is a gate*
Four is a door	*Nine is a line*
Five is a hive	*Ten is a hen*

To remember a fact or piece of information, a student associates it with one of the concrete images. For example, a student might want to remember the following information about ancient Egyptian civilization:

- Egyptian civilization developed along the Nile River in Africa.

- The Egyptians used a system of writing called hieroglyphics.

- The Egyptians built the pyramids as burial places for their pharaohs.

To remember these facts, a teacher may recommend using a mnemonic device—connecting them to the image for number one, a bun. The student could picture a hot-dog bun with the Nile River flowing through the center, hieroglyphics written on the side of it, and pyramids sitting on top of it. The image is easier to remember than the list of facts (Marzano, 2012a, p. 116).

Image Mnemonic

Students use pictures to represent the concept—the sillier the better—to increase retention. An example for the difference between *stalactite* and *stalagmite* might be a drawing of a cave with mites crawling on the ground and tights hanging from the ceiling.

Music Mnemonic

Students use songs or music to remember information. Anyone who tends to sing along with music on the radio probably knows thousands of lyrics. Given a product at the grocery store, a person may remember the jingle that goes with that product. Music and lyrics stick in our memory. One example is the alphabet song, used for young children to remember the alphabet.

Connection Mnemonic

Students use this technique to connect the concept to be learned with something they already know. For example, to remember longitude and latitude, they could connect the *N* in longitude with the *N* in north. Latitude lines must run east to west, because there is no *N* in latitude.

Spelling Mnemonic

Students use this type of mnemonic to help them remember the rules or exception to the rules for spelling words. An example is: *A principal at a school is your pal, and a principle you believe or follow is a rule.*

Link Strategy

Students link symbols and substitutes together in a chain of events or a narrative story. For example, *hydrant* might be a substitute for *hydrogen*. An oxygen tank might be a symbol for oxygen. Two hydrants on top of an oxygen tank would be the mental image for remembering that water is two parts hydrogen and one part oxygen.

Common Mistakes

Here are a few of the common mistakes you might make as you implement mnemonic devices in your classroom:

- The teacher does not instruct students how to create or use a mnemonic device.

- The teacher requires students to create a mnemonic device after the chunk of new information without giving them time to process and elaborate on the concept first.

- The teacher does not provide enough or any time for students to process, summarize, and create a mnemonic device.

- The teacher asks students to create a mnemonic device when it is not an appropriate technique for recording and representing knowledge.

- The teacher provides an inappropriate mnemonic-device format for the type of information to be learned or retained.

Examples and Nonexamples of Mnemonic Devices in the Classroom

As with the previous techniques, you will find two sets of examples and nonexamples (one elementary and one secondary) of how you can use the technique of mnemonic devices in a classroom.

Elementary Example of Using Mnemonic Devices

In this first example, second-grade students are beginning a new unit in science on the role of water in the Earth's surface processes. The learning target is: *Develop a model to represent the shapes and kinds of land and bodies of water in an area* (NGSS Grade 2: Earth's Systems).

> Good morning, class. During this unit, we have been learning about the major bodies of water known as oceans and how important they are to weather and the formation of the Earth over time. Remember, they are Artic, Southern (or Antarctic), Indian, Atlantic, and Pacific. Today, I'm going to give you an easy way to remember the names of the oceans. It's called a mnemonic. To create a mnemonic for the oceans, we are going to take the first letter from each name—**A, S, I, A,** and **P**—and develop a sentence in which the first word will begin with the first letter of one of the oceans. This will help us remember the names of the oceans. I have put an example on the board so you can see what I mean, but you cannot use that one. The sentence is "Apples soak in a pail." The handout I have given you has the ocean names with the first letter underlined. You will work in groups of three to come up with your mnemonic. Once you have it, please write it on the chart paper, and I will put it up on the wall for everyone to see.

The students work on their mnemonics, write them on chart paper, and the teacher posts them. They have a large group discussion about how the mnemonic they created will help them remember the names of the five oceans. After the discussion, students partner up and test each other to see if the mnemonic they developed really did help them remember the five oceans.

Elementary Nonexample of Using Mnemonic Devices

This nonexample uses the same learning target and lesson about the five oceans:

> Good morning, class. During this unit, we have been learning about the major bodies of water known as oceans and how they are important to weather and the formation of the Earth over time. Remember, they are Artic, Southern (or Antarctic), Indian, Atlantic, and Pacific. We are going to create something called a mnemonic. To create a mnemonic for the oceans, we are going to take the first letter from each name—**A, S, I, A,** and **P**—and develop a sentence using those letters to help us remember the names. You will work in groups of three to come up with your mnemonic. Once you have it, please write it on the chart paper, and I will put it up on the wall for everyone to see.

In this example, the teacher is presenting the same activity but does not give much instruction on how to create the mnemonic. She does not give students a guiding worksheet or provide an example of what a mnemonic should look like. Students may be confused and have many questions about what they are exactly supposed to do. The teacher will end up using class time to clarify the instructions and will need to work with the student groups to make sure they understand the activity.

Secondary Example of Using Mnemonic Devices

The secondary example takes place in a high school science class. The students are beginning a unit in life science. The learning target is: *Evaluate the evidence for the role of group behavior on individual and species' chances to survive and reproduce* (NGSS Grades 9–12 Life Science: Ecosystems).

> Good afternoon, class. During this unit, we have been learning about life science and how different species behave, survive, reproduce, and have an impact on other species. We will continue today by using the eight classification categories you learned yesterday and discussing the classification of living things. There are eight categories by which we classify living things—Kingdom, Phylum, Class, Order, Family, Genus,

Species, and Variety. You are going to create image mnemonics to help you remember those eight categories. Remember, an image mnemonic is when you use silly pictures to help you remember a concept. There is an example on the board to remind you. Once you are done, I will give you time to share with a partner.

The teacher gives his students an appropriate amount of time to read the section of the text and create an image mnemonic for each category. He then gives the class about ten minutes to share with a partner and explain how the image mnemonics will help them remember the classification categories. At the end of class, the teacher asks his students to summarize the important points of the lesson by using their mnemonic as the only resource.

Secondary Nonexample of Using Mnemonic Devices

The nonexample uses the same science learning target and lesson, and again, the teacher would like her students to be able to recall the eight classification strategies:

Good afternoon, class. Today, we are going to begin a unit on life science and how different species behave, survive, reproduce, and have an impact on other species. We will start by learning about and discussing the classification of living things. There are eight categories by which we classify living things—Kingdom, Phylum, Class, Order, Family, Genus, Species, and Variety. I would like you to take some time and read about these classification categories in the text. You will need to be able to remember these as we continue through this unit, so you will create an image mnemonic device to help you. After you are finished, we will share some of these devices as a large group.

Determining If Students Can Represent Critical Content with Mnemonic Devices

To move students toward the desired result—in this case, to represent, understand, and retain critical content in an accurate way—monitor all students in the classroom. Once you begin to monitor all students for the desired result, you will immediately know if you have achieved the desired result from this technique. If not all students achieve the desired result, additional support should be put in place to help those students. There are multiple ways to monitor for the desired result of recording and representing knowledge through mnemonic devices.

- Inside-outside circles: The teacher has the students form two circles, one inside circle and one outside circle, and he stands in the middle of the inside circle. Half of the students are in each, and the two circles face each other. The students have a few minutes to share and explain their mnemonic device with the student they are facing in the opposite circle. When the teacher signals, students take three steps to the right and share again with their new partner. The teacher listens to the ongoing discussions and makes sure his students have represented the most important information with their mnemonic devices.

- The three-sentence wrap-up: After instruction, processing, elaborating, and recording and representing have occurred, the teacher asks students to summarize in three sentences or fewer what she taught or presented, using their mnemonic device as their only resource. Students can pair-share their summaries or use them as an exit ticket from class.

Table 6.1 is a student proficiency scale for mnemonic devices. You may need to adapt this to determine how students are progressing in their ability to accurately represent and understand the critical information.

Table 6.1: Student Proficiency Scale for Mnemonic Devices

Emerging	Fundamental	Desired Result
Students create a mnemonic device but cannot use it to remember the big ideas or details of the lesson. Students create a mnemonic device but cannot use it to summarize the critical information in the lesson without help from a peer partner or the teacher.	Students create a mnemonic device and can use it to identify the big ideas but not the supporting details of the lesson. Students create a mnemonic device and can use it to identify some of the big ideas and details in the lesson.	Students can successfully create a mnemonic device and use it to accurately identify the big ideas and details in the lesson. Students are able to explain to their peers and/or teacher how the mnemonic device helps them remember the critical information.

Scaffold and Extend Instruction to Meet Students' Needs

For every technique of recording and representing knowledge this guide has described, there are ways for teachers to both support and extend the technique for the students in their classes. After teachers have monitored their students for the desired result, these supports and extensions are put into place to help those students who need some scaffolding or a bit more of a challenge. This will give students a greater chance of meeting the desired result of the strategy, and more importantly, achieving success in progressing with their learning.

Scaffolding

For those students who need extra support in creating a mnemonic device as a technique for recording and representing knowledge, consider the following suggestions:

- Especially when students are first learning this skill, have them work with a partner. "Two heads are better than one" is probably an appropriate adage when students are asked to create something that will help them learn and remember. Also, teachers might find their students to be more engaged in the activity because it is fun to create mnemonic devices together.

- After students create their mnemonic device and are then expected to summarize what they have learned, provide a sentence starter such as "Today's class was mostly about _____" or "Today, I learned _____."

- To help students remember the different types of mnemonic devices they can create, post examples on the bulletin board and refer to them when you give instructions for an activity.

- In addition to the first model you provided for the whole class, model the process once again for students who are struggling.

Extending

- Suggest that students write a poem or song to help them and their classmates remember critical content.

- Ask one student or a group of students to prepare a lesson to present to the class showing how to use a mnemonic device.

Conclusion

The goal of this book is to enable teachers to become more effective in teaching content to their students. The beginning step, as you have learned in the preceding pages, is to become skilled at helping your students *record and represent knowledge.*

To determine if this goal has been met, you will need to gather information from students, as well as solicit feedback from your supervisor or colleagues, to find someone willing to embark on this learning journey with you. Engage in a meaningful self-reflection on your use of the strategy. If you acquire nothing else from this book, let it be the *importance of monitoring.* The tipping point in your level of expertise and your students' achievement is *monitoring.* Implementing this strategy well is not enough. Your goal is the desired result: evidence that your students have developed a deeper understanding of the content by examining their own reasoning.

To be most effective, view implementation as a three-step process:

1. Implement the strategy using your energy and creativity to adopt and adapt the various techniques in this guide.

2. Monitor for the desired result. In other words, while you are implementing the technique, determine whether that technique is effective with the students.

3. If, as a result of your monitoring, you realize that your instruction was not adequate for students to achieve the desired result, seek out ways to change and adapt.

Although you can certainly experience this guide and gain expertise independently, the process will be more beneficial if you read and work through its contents with colleagues. Use the following reflection and discussion questions during a team meeting or even as food for thought prior to a meeting with your coach, mentor, or supervisor.

Reflection and Discussion Questions

Use the following reflection and discussion questions during a team meeting or even as food for thought prior to a meeting with your coach, mentor, or supervisor:

1. How has your instruction changed as a result of reading and implementing the instructional techniques found in this book?

2. What ways have you found to modify and enhance the instructional techniques found in this book to scaffold and enhance your instruction?

3. What was your biggest challenge, in terms of implementing this instructional strategy?

4. How would you describe the changes in your students' learning that have occurred as a result of implementing this instructional strategy?

5. What will you do to share what you have learned with colleagues at your grade level or in your department?

Resource A

ORGANIZER TEMPLATES

Get the Gist

Name _____

Title _____

Concept/Source _____

1. Critical Information:

    Who:

    What:

    When:

    Where:

    Why:

    How:

2. Write a 20-word GIST summary.

    _____

    _____

    _____

    _____

The Narrative Frame

Read the assigned text and answer the following questions:

1. Who are the main characters, and what distinguishes them from others?

2. When and where did the story take place? What were the circumstances?

3. What prompted the action in the story?

4. How did the characters express their feeling?

5. What did the main characters decide to do? Did they set a goal, and, if so, what was it?

6. How did the main characters try to accomplish their goals?

7. What were the consequences?

Combination Notes

Notes	Pictorial Representation

Summarize your learning:

Analogy Chart

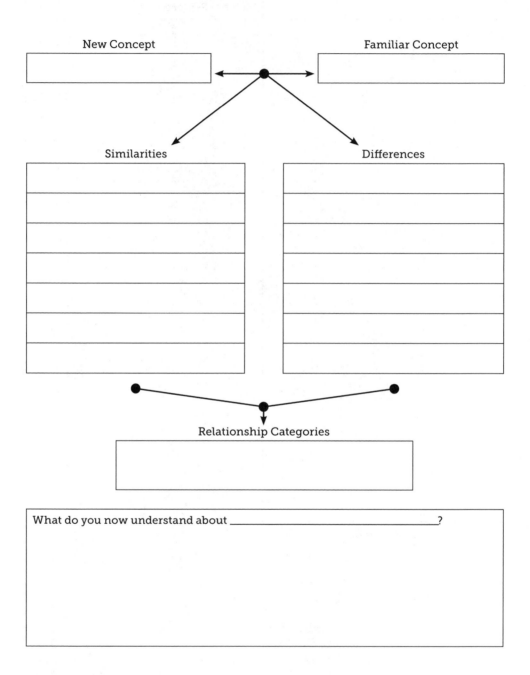

New Concept

Familiar Concept

Similarities

Differences

Relationship Categories

What do you now understand about _____?

Cause/Effect

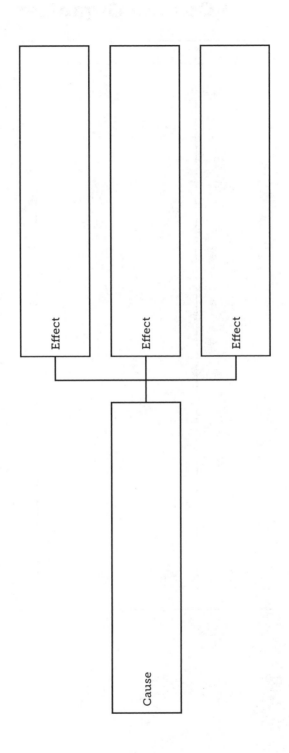

Cause

Effect

Effect

Effect

Column Organizer

Descriptive Pattern

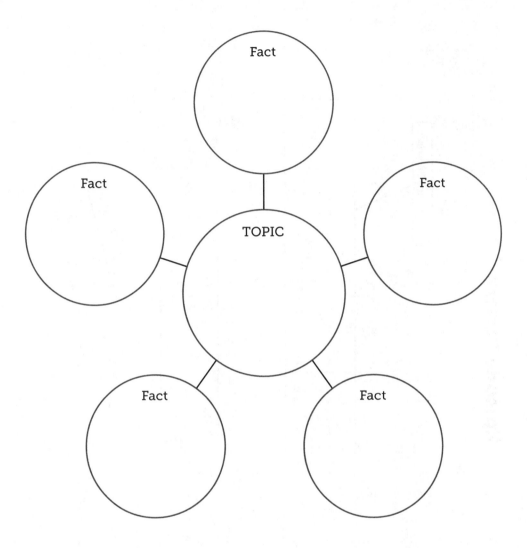

Episode Pattern

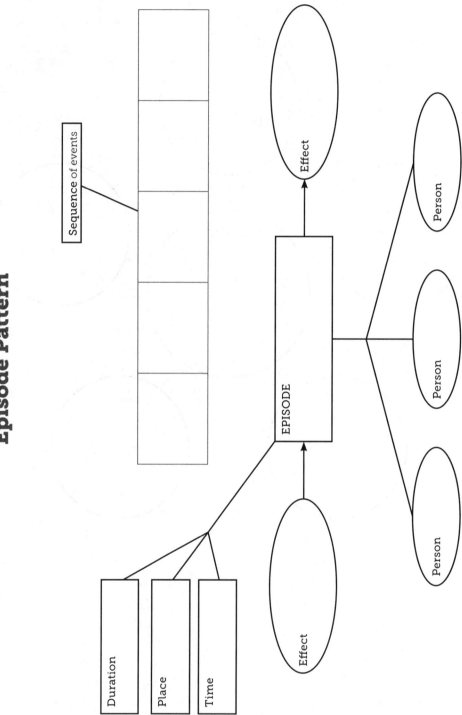

Frayer Model

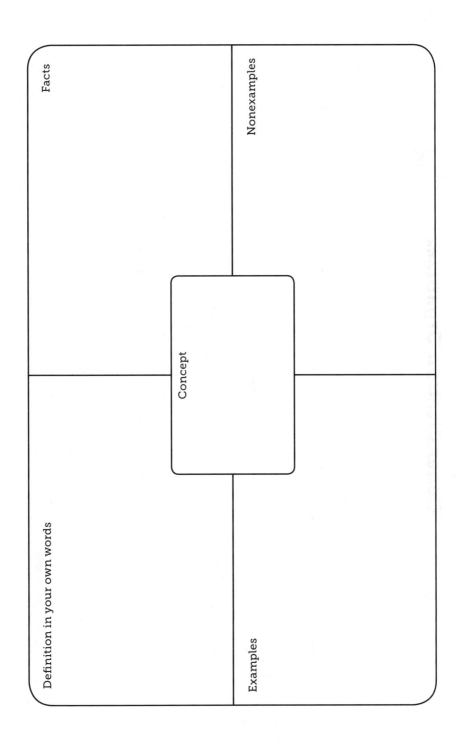

Facts

Nonexamples

Definition in your own words

Concept

Examples

Generalization Organizer

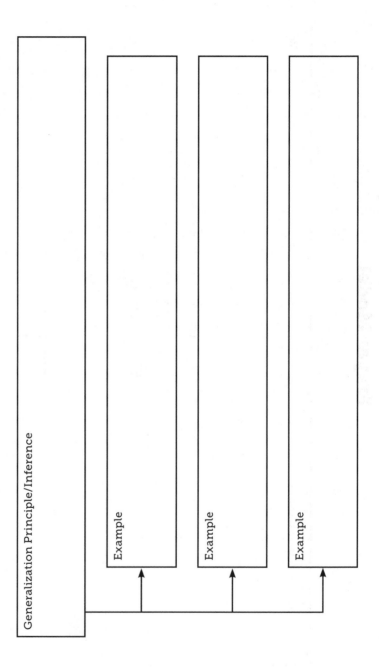

Generalization Principle/Inference

Example

Example

Example

Simple Story Map

Beginning

Middle

End

Time Sequence/Sequence Chain

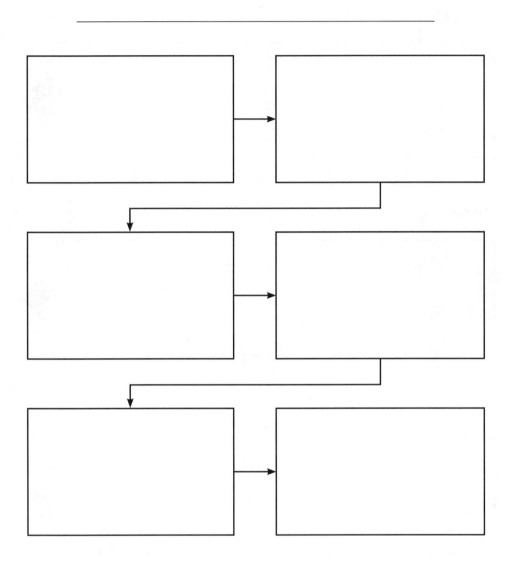

Vocabulary Web

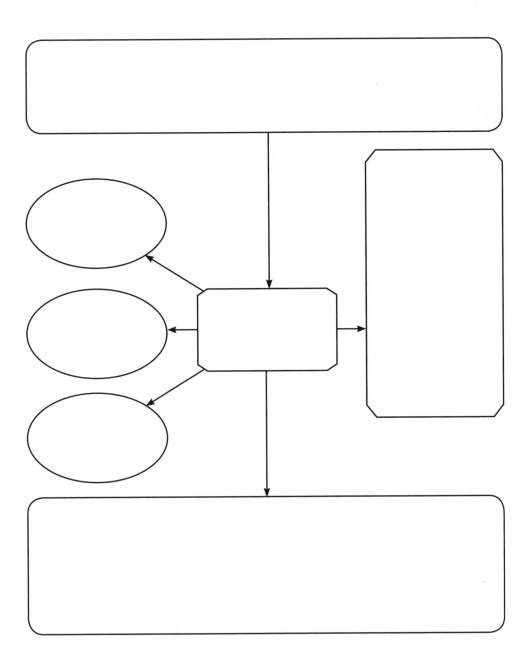

Have a Mnemonics Party

Create a mnemonic device for remembering each piece of information in the selections below. Try making a mnemonic without changing the order and then a few where you reorganize the items to fit your mnemonic.

1. Order of the planets from the sun out – **Mercury, Venus, Earth, Mars, Jupiter, Saturn, Uranus, Neptune, and Pluto.**

    _____

2. Going shopping – **eggs, milk, onions, butter, cucumbers, lettuce, and Tide.**

    _____

3. Bloom's 6 levels of thinking ability – **remembering, understanding, applying, analyzing, evaluating, and creating.**

    _____

4. Reasons why reciting notes aloud increases memory – **gets you involved, provides feedback on what you know, supplies motivation, uses many senses in learning, and promotes concentration.**

    _____

5. Six types of machines – **lever, inclined plane, axle and wheel, jackscrew, pulley, and gear.**

    _____

6. Factors that affect water evaporation – **temperature, area exposed, wind, and humidity.**

    _____

7. Four types of chemical reactions – **synthesis, decomposition, single-replacement, and double-replacement.**

    _____

8. Basic steps in the scientific method – **state the problem, gather information on the problem, form hypothesis, experiment to test hypothesis, record data, analyze date, and draw conclusions.**

    _____

9. General properties of matter – **mass, weight, volume, and density.**

    _____

Adapted from: Congos, D. (2005, January 24). *9 types of mnemonics for better memory.*
Retrieved from http://www.learningassistance.com/2006/january/mnemonics.html

Resource B

HELPFUL WEBSITES

GRAPHIC ORGANIZERS

- *Education Oasis*—Character and Story Graphic Organizers: http://www.educationoasis.com/curriculum/GO/character_story.htm

- *Worksheet Works*—Graphic Organizers: http://www.worksheetworks.com/miscellanea/graphic-organizers.html

- *Thinkport* – Graphic Organizers: http://www.thinkport.org/technology/template.tp

- *Holt* – Holt Interactive Graphic Organizers: http://my.hrw.com/nsmedia/intgos/html/igo.htm

- *Scholastic*—Graphic Organizers for Reading Comprehension: http://www.scholastic.com/teachers/lesson-plan/graphic-organizers -reading-comprehension

- *Houghton Mifflin Harcourt Education Place*—Graphic Organizers http://www.eduplace.com/graphicorganizer/

- *West Virginia Department of Education*—Vocabulary Graphic Organizers: http://wvde.state.wv.us/strategybank/VocabularyGraphicOrganizers.html

- *Cobb County School District*—Graphic Organizers: http://www.cobbk12.org/Cheathamhill/LFS%20Update /Graphic%20Organizers.htm

MNEMONIC DEVICES

- *Mnemonic Devices—*
  http://www.ict4us.com/mnemonics/

- *NASA Cognition Lab—*The Mnemonicizer:
  http://human-factors.arc.nasa.gov/cognition/tutorials/mnemonics
  /index.html

- *Cybrary Man's Educational Web Sites—*Learning Games and Activities and
  Mnemonic Devices:
  http://cybraryman.com/learninggames.html

- *Online Math Learning* Math Mnemonics—
  http://www.onlinemathlearning.com/math-mnemonics.html

DRAMATIC ENACTMENTS

- *Kids' Wings—*Reader's Theater Scripts:
  http://suzyred.com/readerstheater.html

- *Teaching Heart—*Reader's Theater Scripts and Plays:
  http://www.teachingheart.net/readerstheater.htm

VIDEOS

- *Teaching Channel—*Videos of Instruction:
  https://www.teachingchannel.org

References

Anum. (2012a, December 31). How to take notes: Pictorial [Photograph]. *Deducated: The Student Advice Blog*. Retrieved November 24, 2014, from http://deducated. blogspot.com/2012/12/how-to-take-notes-pictorial.html

Anum. (2012b, December 31). How to take notes: Pictorial [Web log message]. *Deducated: The Student Advice Blog*. Retrieved November 24, 2014, from http:// deducated.blogspot.com/2012/12/how-to-take-notes-pictorial.html

Center on Response to Intervention. (2014). The essential components of RTI. Retrieved November 24, 2014, from http://www.rti4success.org/

Common Core State Standards Initiative. (2010a). *Common Core State Standards for English language arts & literacy in history/social studies, science, and technical subjects*. Washington, DC: Author. Retrieved November 24, 2014, from http:// corestandards.org/assets/CCSSI_ELA%20Standards.pdf

Common Core State Standards Initiative. (2010b). *Common Core State Standards for mathematics*. Washington, DC: Author. Retrieved November 24, 2014, from http://www.corestandards.org/wp-content/uploads/Math_Standards.pdf

Congos, D. (2005, January 24). *9 types of mnemonics for better memory*. Retrieved November 24, 2014, from http://www.learningassistance.com/2006/january /mnemonics.html

Dickson, S. V., Collins, V. L., Simmons, D. C., & Kame'enui, E. J. (1998). Metacognitive strategies: Instructional and curricular basics and implications. In D. C. Simmons & E. J. Kame'enui (Eds.), *What reading research tells us about children with diverse learning needs* (pp. 361–380). Hillsdale, NJ: Erlbaum.

Fisher, D., & Frey, N. (2007). *Checking for understanding: Formative assessment techniques for your classroom*. Alexandria, VA: Association for Supervision and Curriculum Development.

Fisher, D., & Frey, N. (2008). *Better learning through structured teaching: A framework for the gradual release of responsibility*. Alexandria, VA: Association for Supervision and Curriculum Development.

Frey, N., Fisher, D., & Everlove, S. (2009). *Productive work: How to engage students, build teamwork, and promote understanding*. Alexandria, VA: Association for Supervision and Curriculum Development.

Goodwin, B. (2011). *Simply better: Doing what matters most to change the odds for student success.* Aurora, CO: Mid-continent Research for Education and Learning.

Graphic organizers. (n.d.). Retrieved November 24, 2014, from http://www.cobbk12.org/Cheathamhill/LFS%20Update/Graphic%20Organizers.htm

Hall, T., & Strangman, N. (2002). *Graphic organizers.* Wakefield, MA: National Center on Accessing the General Curriculum. Retrieved November 24, 2014, from http://aim.cast.org/learn/historyarchive/backgroundpapers/graphic_organizers

Haystead, M. W., & Marzano, R. J. (2009). *Meta-analytic synthesis of studies conducted at Marzano Research Laboratory on instructional strategies.* Bloomington, IN: Marzano Research Laboratory. Retrieved November 24, 2014, from http://www.marzanoevaluation.com/files/Instructional_Strategies_Report_9_2_09.pdf

Heflebower, T., & Marzano, R. J. (2011). *Teaching and assessing 21st century skills.* Bloomington, IN: Marzano Research Laboratory.

Himmele, P., & Himmele, W. (2011). *Total participation techniques: Making every student an active learner.* Alexandria, VA: Association for Supervision and Curriculum Development.

King, A. [Performer]. (2012, August). Farming in the gilded age: A simulation [Web video]. Retrieved November 24, 2014, from https://www.teachingchannel.org/videos/using-simulation-in-the-classroom

Marzano, R. J. (2007). *The art and science of teaching: A comprehensive framework for effective instruction.* Alexandria, VA: Association for Supervision and Curriculum Development.

Marzano, R. J. (with T. Boogren, T. Heflebower, J. Kanold-McIntyre, & D. Pickering). (2012a). *Becoming a reflective teacher.* Bloomington, IN: Marzano Research Laboratory.

Marzano, R. J. (2012b). Writing to learn. *Educational Leadership, 69*(5), 82–83.

Marzano, R. J., & Brown, J. L. (2009). *Handbook for the art and science of teaching.* Alexandria, VA: Association for Supervision and Curriculum Development.

Marzano, R. H., Pickering, D. J., & Pollock, J. E. (2001). *Classroom instruction that works: Research-based strategies for increasing student achievement.* Alexandria, VA: Association for Supervision and Curriculum Development.

Marzano, R. J., & Simms, J. A. (with T. Roy, T. Heflebower, & P. Warrick). (2013a). *Coaching classroom instruction.* Bloomington, IN: Marzano Research Laboratory.

Marzano, R. J., & Simms, J. A. (2013b). *Vocabulary for the Common Core*. Bloomington, IN: Marzano Research Laboratory.

Marzano, R. J., & Toth, M. D. (2013). *Deliberate practice for deliberate growth: Teacher evaluation systems for continuous instructional improvement*. West Palm Beach, FL: Learning Sciences International.

Marzano, R. J., Waters, T., & McNulty, B. A. (2005). *School leadership that works: From research to results*. Alexandria, VA: Association for Supervision and Curriculum Development.

McEwan, E. K. (2007). *40 ways to support struggling readers in content classrooms, grades 6–12*. Thousand Oaks, CA: Corwin Press.

McEwan-Adkins, E. K., & Burnett, A. J. (2013). *20 literacy strategies to meet the Common Core: Increasing rigor in middle and high school classrooms*. Bloomington, IN: Solution Tree Press.

Mnemonic devices. (n.d.). Retrieved November 24, 2014, from http://www.ict4us.com/mnemonics/

National Council for the Social Studies. (2014). *National curriculum standards for social studies: Chapter 2—The themes of social studies*. Retrieved November 24, 2014, from http://www.socialstudies.org/standards/strands

Next Generation Science Standards: For states, by states. (2013). Retrieved November 24, 2014, from http://www.nextgenscience.org/next-generation-science-standards

RTI Action Network. (2014). What is RTI? Retrieved November 24, 2014, from http://www.rtinetwork.org/learn/what

Rutherford, P. (2008). *Instruction for all students* (2nd ed.). Alexandria, VA: Just ASK Publications.

Summary frames. (n.d.). Retrieved November 24, 2014, from http://sddial.k12.sd.us/esa/doc/teachers/marzano/SummaryFrames.pdf

Thinkport. (2014). Graphic organizers. Retrieved November 24, 2014, from http://www.thinkport.org/technology/template.tp

Voltz, D. L., Sims, M. J., & Nelson, B. (2010). *Connecting teachers, students, and standards: Strategies for success in diverse and inclusive classrooms*. Alexandria, VA: Association for Supervision and Curriculum Development.

West Virginia Department of Education. (n.d.). Frayer model. Retrieved November 24, 2014, from http://wvde.state.wv.us/strategybank/FrayerModel.html

Index

A

academic notebooks, 32–33
action verbs to teach, 15–17
analogy chart, 47, 92

B

behaviors, associated with experts, 1

C

cause/effect organizer, 47, 93
CCSS (Common Core State Standards), 3
    defined, 2
CCSSI (Common Core State Standards
    Initiative), 2
chunking, 16, 17
column organizer, 47, 94
combination notes, 31, 91
compacting, 16–17
comprehension, 16, 17
concept map, 47, 51, 52
conceptualizing, 17
connecting, 17
content, defined, 2

D

descriptive organizer, 47, 95
desired result
    See also name of instructional
    technique
    defined, 2
    monitoring, 7–8
dramatic enactments
    common mistakes, avoiding, 69
    description of technique, 67
    examples and nonexamples,
    69–71
    implementation, 67–68
    monitoring for desired result,
    71–72
    scaffolding and extending
    instruction, 72–73
    student proficiency scale, 72
    websites on, 104

E

episode organizer, 48, 96
extending, defined, 2
extending instruction
    See also name of instructional
    technique
    meeting students' needs and, 8–9

F

facilitation, 17–18
Frayer Model, 45, 48, 97
free-flowing web, 31, 35

G

generalization organizer, 48, 98
gist, getting the, 21–22, 89
graphic organizers
    See also type of
    common mistakes, avoiding, 50
    critical attributes of, 44–45
    description of technique, 43
    examples and nonexamples,
    50–55

graphic organizers *(continued)*
    implementation, 43–48
    lesson plan for, 46–47
    listed by text type/content, 49
    monitoring for desired result, 55
    scaffolding and extending
    instruction, 56
    student proficiency scale, 56
    summarizing and, 44
    text frames, 45
    types of common, 47–48
    websites on, 103

I

implementation process, 85
independent reading, 19–20
informal outlines, 30, 37
instructional strategies, defined, 2
instructional techniques
    See also name of instructional
    technique
    defined, 2
    description of, 10–11

K

knowledge, recording and representing
    implementation tips, 6–8
    mistakes, common, 6–7
    teacher actions or behaviors
    needed for implementing, 6

L

linguistic representations
    note taking, 29–40
    summarizing, 15–28

M

Marzano, R. J., 1
    instructional framework, 2–3

mnemonic devices
    common mistakes, avoiding, 78
    description of technique, 75
    examples and nonexamples,
    78–81
    examples for creating, 102
    implementation, 75–78
    monitoring for desired result, 82
    scaffolding and extending
    instruction, 83–84
    student proficiency scale, 83
    types of, 75–78
    websites on, 103–104
modeling, 15
    See also name of instructional
    technique
monitoring
    See also name of instructional
    technique
    defined, 2
    desired result, 7–8

N

narrative frames, 22, 90
Next Generation Science Standards, 3
nonlinguistic representations
    dramatic enactments, 67–73
    graphic organizers, 43–56
    mnemonic devices, 75–84
    pictorial notes and pictographs,
    57–65
note taking
    academic notebooks, 32–33
    combination notes, 31, 91
    common mistakes, avoiding,
    33–34
    description of technique, 29
    dual-format, 30–33
    examples and nonexamples, 34–38
    free-flowing web, 31, 35
    implementation, 29–33
    informal outlines, 30, 37

monitoring for desired result, 38–39

scaffolding and extending instruction, 39–40

student proficiency scale, 39

teacher-designed templates, 30

O

opportunities, importance of providing ongoing, 6–7

P

pictorial notes and pictographs

common mistakes, avoiding, 59

description of technique, 57–58

examples and nonexamples, 59–63

implementation, 58

monitoring for desired result, 63

scaffolding and extending instruction, 64–65

student proficiency scale, 64

R

readers' theater, 67

reflection, allowing students time for, 7

rigor, essentials for achieving, 3

role play, 68

S

scaffolding

See also name of instructional technique

defined, 2

student needs and, 8–9

self-reflection, teacher, 9–10

simulations, 68

somebody-wanted-but-so-then (SWBST), 21

story map, 48, 99

summarizing

action verbs to teach, 15–17

common mistakes, avoiding, 22

description of technique, 15

examples and nonexamples, 23–26

graphic organizers and, 44

implementation, 15–22

lesson plans for, 18–19, 20

monitoring for desired result, 26–27

prompts and processes for, 21–22

scaffolding and extending instruction, 27–28

student proficiency scale, 27

summary frames, 22, 90

T

text frames, 45

time sequence/sequence chain/chain of events organizers, 48, 100

Toth, M. D., 1

V

vocabulary web, 48, 53–55, 101

Notes

Notes

Notes

MARZANO CENTER

Essentials for Achieving Rigor SERIES

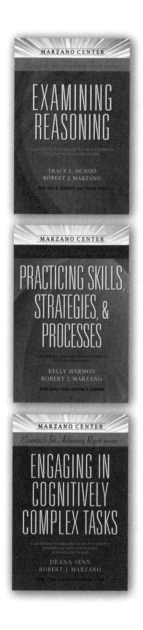

LearningSciencesInternational

LEARNING AND PERFORMANCE MANAGEMENT

Visit www.education-store.learningsciences.com or call 877-411-7114